My
Opened
Chest

My Opened Chest

YON ETHRAIM FEARSHAKER

To order additional copies of this book, contact:
Xlibris LLC
1-888-795-4274
www.Xlibris.com
Orders@Xlibris.com
635470

CONTENTS

IN MEMORIAM

We, Mary Nemeth's sons and daughters, extend a warm welcome to you, her friends and relatives, in this hour of grief. We thank you for the moments you gladdened our mother's heart. The years haven't whittled away your love for her. The various memories you hold of her warm the hearts of us, her children. Death is a strange reaper. It opens doors that should be shut. It closes doors that should be opened. But the hurricane of our mother's love brings a calm to each of us.

As a poor farmer's wife, our mother knew what it was to rise early in the morning with a song of praise to God upon her lips and, upon retiring at night, to give thanks to God for the strength to endure.

To each of you here, I would like to touch your memory of our mother. Although it is not necessary, our mother deserves a bit of commendation for the way she cooperated with her Creator.

MY MOM

She was a little woman with a giant's heart.
She could laugh as loud as those she found laughing.
She could cry as hard as those who were weeping.
She would listen to gossip as if it were enjoyable,
But in the end she would defend the one gossiped about.

She hated injustice
And would defend the truth with all her might.
She enjoyed innocent trickery
But would be the most hurt
If she hurt another.

Those she loved, she expected love in return.
Those she disliked
She gave them room to come into her heart.
She wasn't hyped up on churchgoing,
But she dearly loved the Trinity.

She taught all her children values
And taught it by the life she led
That the greatest value was love.
She taught that no one is beyond redemption.
That's why she had such a forgiving heart.
She loved to sing hymns
And taught us of the joys in heaven.

MY OPENED CHEST

In greet I smiled the day,
The day to open the chest
Lain to attic's dust so long,
Long, long, many years long.

Bust the lock holding stay;
Keys forgotten
In other secret passageway.
In busting eyes
And frigid ear,
My hands, my hands,
So mashed in clay,
Dazed in trembling sweating palm,
Must I, must I make this day
Treble in happy psalm.

Opened chested lid in rust,
Trembling feet unsteady 'neath,
This body's love for lust
In smells of yester's leaf.

Fainting pupils in windowsills,
Melting wax from frigid ears,
Paled my watered palms
As treasured load
Threw my piercing trills
From attic dust
To present 'larms.

I saw ancestral spirits lain
Neath every well-placed,
Well-kept treasure sane,
Thoughtfully laid not by haste,
Under chested lid's
Moldy windowpanes.

Dauntless to mental flushing rain,
I fingered boldly items mean:
Why hinged jar of wheaten grain?
Why wilted stalk of grassy green?
Why buttress rung of chapel chair?
Why trouser of missing leg?
Why this lock of whited hair?
Why this bugle of missing sound?
Why lay this cheating cloth
O'er a pillow of down?
Why this holey glove, so soft?

Why this,
Why that?
Why must reason
Frown at this dark loft
Treasured in mind, many days?
Why, O why,
Did I break the stays
To my chest
In attic's dust?

MY JAR OF GRAIN

The whip-poor-will calls
From the spring-filled stream
Though he of one voiced call
Makes this face all beam.

The whip-poor-will calls
O'er the ripe, mellow fields,
Rippling and waving
To the wind taunt strings,
Singing wheaten harvest song.

The whip-poor-will calls,
And I, aged, must obey
As I trade my scythe
For a hinged jar
Filled with wheaten grain.

The whip-poor-will chants
To plover dove on wing:
There'll be others
To plow my field,
There be others
To walk my stream,
All barefooted hind,
The falling drill.

If there be others
To lift the lid
From my hinged jar
Of wheaten grain,
I'd will them
To finger each grain
And weigh this life I've lived
Down by the whip-poor-will's spring.

There be others
Down by my spring
To sip its waters,
To list its call:
Life is love sewn therein,
Therein this wheaten grain
In hinged sweet jar
Of whip-poor-will.

A WILTED STALK OF GREEN

Somewhere midst this life's mist
Drags my beggared anchor
O'er heaps of unmeasured bliss
Towards this soul's canker,
Looking beyond the windows
Of this body's lifting mist.

Somewhere beyond those windows
Shines a dream for me, ever fair.
Oh, if I could touch that curtain
Making these eyes hazy, Oh so pale,
Wouldst I, with youthful leap,
Reach that dream so real
And grasp that prize without fail?

Somewhere raindrops' begin,
I'll bathe in that pool of mist
And smile my very best grin
To that spirit
Whose lips I've kissed.

Someday I'll find my fields of green;
I'll soak this toiling soul,
And my litter will quickly wean
To more lovely cloth of voile.
Laced in und and 'tween,
My body in newfound faille.

I'll drop my stalk of wilted green
In other hope chest rusted in toil.
I'll hang my hat on head so clean
And walk to my pots of broth,
Singing a song, ever mine.

Throw that wilted stalk
To others midst the mist;
Surely their road shall fork
To better days they've missed.

BUTTRESS RUNG OF CHAPEL CHAIR

Should we join all hands
In ceremonial ring
And toss our jewels in common heap
To salutiferous ingenious feast
Whilst the heart keeps a gem
Ashy from the common heap?

We, in after dine,
Watch each heart in skipped beat
Pick its jewel in mental theft
Back to self from common heap.

We sit in this great gazebo,
Plucking the petal bloom
From sweet, pretty daisy flower
As we, in our know,
Chase words into gloom.

We find each self holds the seeds,
The only the seeds of sweet daisy head,
And wish back our petals of bloom,
Given to unison's call.

We hush our melee of words
Once the bane self-desires
Rush our souls with swordsy hands
To fill our sacred gazebo
With the ashes of the common heap.

Each finds his jewel in heap
Shines less than hour before
Till one of hearty soul
Knocks the chair askew
And holds in hand the words,
Belying the common heap.

He, though in words none,
Takes the buttress rung
From our chapel chair
As we in soul come to know
'Tis the buttress rung,
Not our chapel chair,
Writing answer on soul.

A TROUSER OF MISSING LEG

I smiled one day
To a happy small man
Plying his work without delay
To me as on my road I ran.

I knew not this happy small man
Plying his wares on shabby van,
Nor cared I picked his wordy wand
As on my reed I ran.

I walked a mile
Side the happy small man
Syllabling words, just words to me,
As I pushed my gait
On my road as I ran.

I turned quickly aside
And said, "One thing answer me,
You happy small man
Plying your wares in shabby van,
First I've my road to go
Fore I can say I've ran.
Why trouble you, my road so,
With your empty, shabby van?"

I walked my road in silence
Side this small but happy man
Fore his thunder crossed my road
As onwards I ran.

I stopped midway,
This road of small happy man,
Peeked his empty shabby van
As my eyes cried to brain
On this road I ran.

I took back my gait
And opened my mouth in word,
"Answer me,
You small but happy man,
Why paint the last judgment
On floor of shabby van?"

I looked this road I ran
And saw my small but happy man
Plying his wares
Whilst wearing trouser,
A trouser of missing leg,
Troubling this road on which I ran,
My course on goodly two,
Yet not plying my wares
Nor happy with smile,
Just running with empty hand
On this road as I ran.

BUGLE OF MISSING SOUND

Friendly lips whisper a song to me,
To me, a sing-sing song, oversung,
To gestures rolled in monologue
And lips' half-pardoning words.
Forgive me, friend, those words spoke
By yesterday's well-meant joke;
I'm deaf, if you would know.

Mine ears now failed
This ship nonswayed in billowed mast,
Forgets its wake, its telltale path,
Long fore color returns to sea
And striking waves crash the bow,
Seem as christening hour.

How's this bow to turn in journey, half,
In remembrance of yester's wake?
For some word hung in half-laugh
As the morrow promises a flake
Melting in ego bath.

Walk this deck of ghosting ship
And list the sounds of night watch
Played by the bugler's lip,
Having ears of nonsounding notch;
Though his fingers blithely slip
O'er the holes of missing note.

Sit beside my bugler's chair,
List the bugle of missing sound
Played by deaf bugler's share.
Ponder that heart, which doth pound
Within this bugler's solitude.

Though the song's without word,
There's music within that body hewed
Forth to hear the flight of bird
As issued from the bugle renewed
In the mind of deaf man, heard.

When the angel legions
Sound their bugles in flight,
Do place this bugle, missed of sound,
Neath the lid of chested regions
For angels hear in crested heights.

HOLEY GLOVE

Down by the junket
Breathing sounds of smell
As tide in strength sunk it
To black bottom downed
In silt of worn creation's kit.

That wharf seethes in sorrow
Suckled by barnacled weight,
Grossly endured by the sow
Of tides in and out of moon gate.

Painfully, piteously in sorrowed tow,
That junket of raised ghost
Kneads a bread of new dough
For future sea engrossed
To battle a junket of battened bow.

Sitting in captain's chair
All bristled for command,
Sways a salty brow
Above locks of whited hair
In deepened thought
Of chastised waves,
Foaming far from land.

This salty brow winks at me
With wrinkled, sinewy hand.
He waves at me on wharf by sea,
This stranger loving none but sand.

A crooked and shaky finger
Bids me enter that sacred domain
Kept by none but he in linger,
Reads his mental, worn book again
To me in smell of salty timber.

He talks with swim of hand,
Entrancing me to booty book,
As he alone saw the word of page.
I, in stampeding mind, forsook
My loath of sea for sand.

His hand, nontired by waving wand,
Clothed in worn, much-holed glove,
Spoke to me his things of fond
And the taled sea he did love.

In shattering, chattering shout,
His hand he thrust before my face
For me to see what sea's all about
In that glove holed in grace.

TUMBLEWEEDS

Spirits on their desert horses
Visit the ways of the wind that tosses,
A mind and the thoughts it bosses,
Before a legion erects the crosses
In a soil too poor for mosses,
Poisoned by riderless horses.

On, on, on, a sand is sifted
Until a whirlwind has lifted
The thoughts and mores all drifted
From nature's plan as listed,
Until the tumbleweeds have wilted
A song towards the rider all tilted.

Tumbleweeds, like tumbled hearts,
Roll with the winds until there parts
That certain sting of love's tossed darts
When the eye in wanton starts
Picks all the cherries from the tarts,
Beginning again that tumbleweed heart.

DAWN AS TWILIGHT

Worry not the sands
Where thy toes have left
Their print in image
Through deep or faint stride.
Others will tread 'pon
Your castles in sand,
Holding in mind's eye
How your fort is built.

The seeds of mustard,
Each not of same hue
Nor of roundness same,
Holds under each shell
The knowledge of self.

Worry not the sands
Of all men good-willed;
They, trustworthy seed,
Harbor world's main wheel,
Threshing kernels mien,
Their gruel all wiser
By siftings of will.

Worry not the sands
Where thy toes have left
Many blunders wrought,
Wheeled in gossip's maw
Through threshing unclean.

The cherry has seed
E'er fore blossom burst,
Dare one say not true
Fore its wisdom seen.

Worry not the sands
Where thy toes have left
No minted image
For this seed called you.

The sand remains sand
'Til shapely molded
By all forces nigh.
Might someday the toes
Crescendo its blame.

Worry not the sands
Where thy toes have left
Their loving mishaps
Cautioned in wisdom's
Unruled, unmapped maze.

Remember always,
Those toes speak of you.
Will, in kingdom come,
Those toes shake the dews
From all eyes blinded,
Rushing to your mews.

LAY ME DOWN

Lazy daisies by the roadside bloom,
Careful not where children born,
Just blooming on in days'
Bright sunny or stormy light,
Drinking sap from crying clouds,
Catching rivulets from the road,
Building sandcastles o'er their toes.

Lazy daisies by the roadside bloom,
Smiling an ever blooming smile,
Welcoming bees playing in hair
As tiny feet tickle the crown,
Gathering dandruff all around,
Nursing breasts und the down.
Swooning pistil's hungry lips,
Swelling womb in the hips,
Fading maiden's pretty dress
In exhaustion withering away,
Making place in future's sun
For other children at play.

WITH REGRETS AND ANGER

O hand-waving mobs!
Bring down your sky to earth!
The world's on the brink
With its crushing, rushing race for arms!
O cuss the tank of taxes
Given not for these alarms!
There's a devil in the house
Confusing rightful thought,
Laughing at the mob as a tiny held-up mouse!

O shouting peoples in the streets!
Lobby 'gainst the lobbyists' rule,
Making war out of peace!
And the poor man has not sweets
While the drums of nations drum their mournful beats!
And disease of human flesh
Spray the air with stinking reeks!

O gathering souls to savior-falling crowns!
Walk all day and run all night!
Push your prayers while none the others sleep!
Wake your leader while he's fully awake!
Save the world for cause of waking's sake!

O stillen peoples at the gates?
Staring tanks and bullets' scare?
Came you not with bombs and missile hiss!
Shake you! Shake you the fear behind those guns!
The grave holds not your longing souls!
Nor do moments hold long where bravery's at stake!
Wave your hands high in thrill!
Shout forth the weight of God's own will!
Tumble those walls of maggots' will!
Triggered fingers will pry your will.
Wave your hands, you're unarmed still!

WEEPING SAVAGELY

Dark as a dungeon,
Deep as a cavern;
Vacant as a prebought grave,
Lonely as death's moment.
Darkened in eugenics' cry,
Deeply cut by nature's knife.
Gone other-where,
Winging in Spirit's bath,
Crying to kindly foam
Honed in words unkind
Locale shied, unfit,
Dried to God's own tears.

Foam-smothering unknown hurts,
Flanked by admonished rock
O'ergrown in team sweat
'Cause no one cared.

Melted in homing sands
Down by ledge to sea,
Hypnotic waves' unicall
Come my worth, you'll see.

Waves outdistance the cry,
The cry of vacant mother's arms,
But waters by ledge of sea
Carry her crying tears
To world's all climes,
Peoples, and songs.

None those stringing instruments
Nor reeding pipes she'll have;
Only, if only, she had glimpsed
This moment of vacant arms.

Parents: poor, dumb
Lovers of sonny me
Sing no songs in hum
Of teachery's teach, wee,
Find myself
In garden kinders.

In my garden, kinders,
All mindly eyed in amaze,
Wonder why my lovers
Couldst not fondle days
In teach of sonny me.

In my garden kinders
Making me spicy crook,
I fondle
Paint, brush, and scissors
Hid at home from me.

Seven years of basic me
In home of foster teach
Yet wonder
Why my lovers
Couldst not teach sonny me.

Answered wonder
Came plain to me
At knighted junior feast,
Lack-o-blunder
Takes more than lovers three
To kindle garden kinder's
Bold, bold society.

"Ne'er, ne'er," I whispered in cry,
"Extinguish that candle lit,
Lit in flames,
Moths' love,
Just for sonny me."

BETWEEN THE WARS

Six scores and three years ago,
After the battle clashed in began,
The troll grows lazy
  at Lexington;
The grape's in need of prune
  at Concord.
The summer's neither hot nor cold
  at Sumter;
The fields lie vast and waste
  at Appomattox.
Richmond and Atlanta
  burn in the steam of fate
While those soldiers dressed
  in red or blue and gray
Weep,
Still weep from the grave,
That the garden of America
Could not be plowed
  by none but blood,
Nor could the world
  such nobility fit
To end all wars
Pestering the sojourn of man.
Yet peace is the thread
  Between the wars.

THE PLAIN VIEW

If a country's in need of a leader
and no one to plead the whip,
of what use is a tiresome seeder
with no one to prune the tip?

If a leader proves good to bag
and all are evil to his say,
will his usefulness dog-baying prove as gag
as a fearful dog at its bay?

When all of speech grow old,
therefore shall be wherefore as thereupon
the walls of greening moss to mold
shall be the be works in the will was done,
mattering not the leader's scold?

SPES ANGELORUM

Broaden the rays that are set upon your horizons and, with cautionary trepidity, pull gently the cords of each emotion's strength, perhaps, gone into some tomorrow's closet of fools. Never make yourself sedate in some mysterious thought that another, more-than-brilliant ray of tomorrow's joy sprout sprinkled with the hatred someone else has found in an emotion hoped for but, in a bubble's momentary burst, has escaped the real and truer path to endeavor.

Remember, always, the pith stored in the age's trust that somehow or another, if perchance your searching eyes have not read or your heart has engendered not the sing-outs from ancient wisdoms of writ, there be worn a knitted garment upon your shoulders that time gone by in your self is capable to wash or mend each stain- or strain-broken thread put by life to you; and you yourself, if so desirous enough, can recycle those wash waters of strains, emotions, and fallen down bridges preventing tomorrow's sure-baked bread, is latent and real as the coming morn's sunshine to awaken your whole world from the darkness soon to fade into a destiny that only you, yourself, can control.

AFTER REHEARSAL

The nerves are touchy as drunk on wine;
The real things come, and there's a whine:
"I'm not rehearsed with polish and shine,
Close the curtains just for a little time."
Elaine's the winter and springing like sin;
She views the comics and sages with a grin,
Faceting their faces with an uncut gem
While the dancers and players pound the gold.
She shouts to them, "Hey, get more bold!"
She appears like silly and mimic to sight
All because there's joy in this night.
She stops all things and says a sermon's worth,
"All this song, joy, and mirth
Would fade at the curtain before its birth
If wires and lights and props died in sin
Because the masks on face and clothes were too thin."

The curtain opens to variety in our world,
Singing to the simple joys within,
When the body's great move awakes the din
After the rehearsal removes all but one sin.
As Lucille, in grief, showers a sleazy grin
To her vow-split husband and children so thin,
Her barman friend breaks into a happy smile;
He's happy Lucille didn't go the last mile.
Elaine is pouty but happy within.
The audience laughed at this great sin.

After rehearsal and the play has ended,
All nerves are calmed in a glass of gin,
Then in comes Elaine to the party loud;
She smiles and thanks this professional crowd.
She takes a glass, and in hand it breaks
To Laura singing in high C stakes.
Elaine, with a tear on lid and eyes not dry,
Whispered in song, "I cannot say you did not try."

MISS GISH

She's Miss Gish, and I'd
like you to mind your English,
although she's not above an ish
when speaking to one acting a fool,
        but dare the fool to be near
a pool
for Miss Gish will call him
poolish.
        Miss Gish has been around
for an eon it seems
nigh unto five womb openings
have shared her sliding dreams,
        but oh, oh, oh, and oh,
woe, woe, woe, and woe,
she can still make the words flow,
so don't go near the pool
or act like a fool;
        she's sure to use her loving heart,
and her smile
will tumble you into the pool's fool.
        A lovely lady, always she's been,
up at morning,
        eating a wheat thin,
broadly smiling that American grin;
        but don't touch her clothes
or rub your itchy nose,
she'll think you're less a rose
but still pluck you in a pose.

She's capable to take all around the bend,
to sup on cheese and pungent gin,
but don't tell her statistics lie;
she still knows a fact
that whiskey is only made of rye.
    Shout to her ditties and lines all
crossed with flowing wits.
She'll count for you each and all her biddies;
she's left her mark nigh in all the world's cities
    yet remains as that American belle,
Miss Gish is the name's tell.
    She gives of herself in the acting world
for the poor, the rich, the maimed, and meek
to broaden their minds and teach the reach
that self is seen without its preach
and heaven is not as Mr. Creech would teach.
    She remains the American belle,
Miss Lillian Gish, her name surely tells.
    That's why I would herald,
"You're still my right kind of girl."

SPRING HAS SPRUNG

There's a desire to walk in the wood
To hear pulpit Jack proclaim, "It's spring."
And all the realm acts as it should
While listening to bluebells ring.

Robins and bluebirds,
Jonquils with trumpets ablared,
Azaleas with colorful words,
And Lady Violet nodding so fair
As Master Wind tussle's her hair.

The sun warms to this show
As maple ribbons her dress
And tulip gossips are a-flow
While crocus are practicing incest
Beside anemone's ferny bower.

All nature from sleet and snow
Greedily welcome spring's blushed shower
As blades of grass in hopeful show
Race blossoms without cower.
This the season sprung to know
Each small worm and beautied flower.

This the season man's so small
With his science and knowledge tall
While in the spring God throws his paints
And shouts, "Where there is will, there're no ain'ts,"
As spring yells in reply,
"Glory to you, O God, on high."

FALLEN FIGS

INHERITABLES

Pretty things don't last forever;
Their value is short-lived or so.
Years determine their scope
Until child of child brings another eye
To blind the sentimental touch.

Across the years, fourth child or so,
Begins a search into yesterday;
Those pretty things are gone forever,
Away from the touch of ancestral tree,
Too blind for sentiment's touch.

The child of children's children
Makes again those pretty things
In rivalry of yesterday's touch,
But gone again to sentiment's chest
Until blood seeks the bond of flesh
Once again to smiles and tears.

PANGS

The talons are set,
The wings folded in flight;
The prey beats an unknown path,
Its way is not to this night.

The wings unfold
To talons long set;
The prey is too near home,
Its heart forgets the fright.

Talons, wings, and feathers
Mass to the bloody fall;
The prey stops as still as death,
Talons, wings, and feathers
      Breathe last breath.

A SOJOURN

Where the seas
     of life merge
Into the oceans
     of thought,
Its ship is listing
     in waves, emerged,
The shore;
     though not distant,
     seems so ill wrought.

POLITICS

Like a rat in a maze
Looking for an unchanged change
Are us humans treading telltale paths,
Thinking leaders are lies' lied change,
Until the leader of the public trust
Leaves the streetwalker to learn its maze.

IN CREATE

Dogs bark
      to give their prey a chance.
Cats sneak;
      they favor not a prolonged dance.
In summation, it's all the same—
What one lacks, nature's sure to enhance.
Until the day of reckoning comes,
Both must yield to degenerative stance
Lest one finds mental powers of trance
The better than prideful prance.

INTIMIDATION

To the walls of endeavor all are called,
Whether by feign or strength or gall;
The feigning seek no remorse,
The strengthened seek not the rubber balled.
Those of gall cry into intimidation's pot,
Yet all seek the same as got.

ALL EVEN SIDES

As the poor cry to the rich,
So does the rich cry to the poor.
If the poor were not poor
And the rich were not rich,
Where are the friends
      Come knocking on the door end?
Where are the laborers to dig man's ditch?

THE SCABBARD

When a forest is cut for fuel,
It's not cut for uselessness.
When a cabbage is cut for food,
It's not cut down for uselessness.
When a person is cut for another's pride,
It is cut for uselessness;
Thus, there's more to a scabbard
      Than the leather which hides.

THE GATHERING

Trade a blossom for a seed
If the blossom comes from weed;
On the blossom the weed shall feed,
Dumping seed for a taste of greed.
Though the blossom shall lie to bleed,
The seed shall blossom to succeed,
Leaving other blossom's rightful deed
If with weed it does not plead.

ICON SEEK

Engraved gods and images
No longer grace the house of man;
The bell thus rung
Speaks not a better generation come.

The mind has grown,
The bend's lazed by eye,
No longer needs engraved images
To hold the worth of heart's desire.

We see by feel
The lips' spoken word;
Thus engraved images
Become ornaments of mind,
Changed by fomented curl of tongue
Into a traveled path of rate.

HUNTING TIME

When the corn tassels and coon know its time,
When the carrots scent the air
      and the rabbit knows its path,
When the beans are dressed in bloom
      and the beetles hear the tune,
That's when I open hunting time.

Though the coon cutes its face,
Though the rabbit pulls at heart,
Though the beetles bless its host,
Though it's I in wasted labor,
Know it's open hunting time.

A roast may suit the coon,
A stew may suit the rabbit,
A fluid may suit the beetle,
A tear may flood my eye,
A feast is on my table
In thanks for a garden grown
Because I knew it was hunting time.

THE POND OF REED

Ah, wonderful thing indeed
To see faith's time seed
Growing as a youthful weed
In this hour of need.

Remember those times of intercede
When others asked your mind to heed
The kind of dough you knead
Along the path your life would lead
You into your pond of reed.

Now that love of gentle feed
Mingles with your same creed
In ask of you to precede,
Grasping true love's greed
As the flesh does not impede
The love of friend in heart bleed,
Watching the hour of time's bead
And wishing you Godspeed.

Godspeed, my friend, into God's need;
Your hour of trial will not recede
The waves upon your pond of reed.
This hour is guaranteed
For soul to live and plead
Your growth of faithful seed
Down by your pond of reed.

A SUMMER'S BLIZZARD

Dust,
      Heat,
            Sweat,
Women with powder coagulated in pools;
Men with salt rags a-dripping,
Dogs with tongues as open faucets,
Dribbling on master's thirsty Sunday's best.

Dust,
      Heat,
            Sweat,
Cats clawing into bird veins;
Birds weighted with mud from cracked dry creek.
Utilities gone pleading for ration,
Fans whirring for one cool blast.

Dust,
      Heat,
            Sweat,
The violets' seed is drying;
One match pollutes the air,
Only a spring keeps from dying
The thoughts of every tongue.

PICKING FROM THE FIELD

All our troubles are samples of thought
Picked from the many-hued fields
Tasted on the battle lines, self-imposed,
Thrown to others not willed to consensus
While the battle ceases not within
Until the senses withdraw in retreat:
I'm not only one in thought.

Thought must have its presence spent
Behind the palisade fence
Before the reaper shouts to victory,
Before the thought becomes the peace,
Before trouble ceases its pendulumed race
Tearing through the many-hued fields.

THE NURSING FEET

There's a lovely sound
      no other can match;
'Tis the sound of feet
      drumming the tile,
A cadence without a beat,
Spasmodic the rhythm,
      enthralling its rest
When lips hush a bleat.
Then off again
      in unrhythmic beat,
Like a crushing mouse
In rush some morsel to eat;
Then hushed again
      at mission house.

When a soul takes to trumpet,
Blasting the slowness of beat,
The tile path mirrors
      two much busy feet
As if to prayer
      one petition, long.

Where, oh where,
Shadow, shadow,
      through the mirrored tile,
Is reality an unrhythmic while,
Gone chasing a frown
      to dress a face with smile.

THE ZODIACS CRY

Gone is a time when sorcerers had their sway,
Today they only charge and get in the way;
There's nothing they would do without a pay—
Not even a piece of light on a ray
To open a gush in broad, open day.

They say they have their sway day by day
To those following zodiac's essay.

There comes a time when caves are nest, foray,
Only squawks and dribbles on stacked-up clay.

THE TICKING OF A GONG

There are numbers to be remembered
      and hearts to break asunder—
How many times is I love you?

There are houses to be numbered
      and clothes to be worn;
How many times does love have to be washed?

There's water to run over the dam
        and floods to wash the eve;
How many times does a tear wash down?

There're babies to die and to be born
        and streets to be made and worn;
How many times does a child have to laugh?

Marriage and death to grave way down
        And heaven to hell, never a sound;
How many times is death in a tub?

How many times is I love you?
How many times does love have to be washed?
How many times does a tear wash down?
How many times is death in a tub?
How many times,
        How many times,
                How many times.

ADVERTISE

If women shy your company,
        advertise.
If women are more than your company,
        advertise.
If company is not your company,
        advertise.
If you can't ladder in your company,
        advertise.
If friends are untrue out of company,
        advertise.
If friends are true in your company,
        advertise.

If life is your company,
       advertise.
If death comes to your company,
Let others advertise.

THE REST IS ABED

We worry our heads
       for the day that is;
We trouble the day to come.
We have not faith that was his;
We stumble the equation
       as one that's dumb.

The day that is will surely end;
The day that will be may dawn.
Man has not power to bend
       nature into a pawn.

Go your way and sing the beat;
Hold the tune for tomorrow's song.
The night shall come for noble rest
In dreams for the future's song.

ON READING A BOOK

Deeds are like a book;
The cover shouts louder
       than the print.

Words are all the same
Until their place in sentence
       is fixed.

The interrogative mark
       points in and out
Until a deed finds directions
              of shout,
Then the interrogative mark
Points from earth to heaven,
From heaven to earth.
Nice day it is
       to show one's worth.

Tales lose their hair
When voice is frozen in print;
It takes one with care
To thaw its reason sent.

Facts are all the same,
       voiced or otherwise;
It takes a stretcher or a vice
       To really change their size.

There are some facts
       that cannot be changed;
Though meddled with or pried,
They remain, only rearranged.

   To a BIRTHDAY

Stomp your feet,
       feel good solid earth;
Clap your hands,
       hear the wind part in song.
See the grasses and worm beneath;
Taste the fields
       after blossom set.

Sprinkle your lips
      with hyssop herb,
Wag the tongue
      belonging not to self.
This is your birthday.

A VOICE IN THE FOG

Where the soil and horizon meet,
Many the tales and eternal long
The drums' ethereal beat;
Rainbows meld their colors without song,
Dreams weigh life's retouchable sheet,
Reality sails the seas to right and wrong
While the Maker juggles a feast.

THE WORTH OF A WORD

Transport my cause
      and misquote me not;
My words may not be
      for momented bird,
But surely, as the night
      draws into another day,
The shelf will loathe to hold
Those words once thrown away.

The flesh man tastes
      that rippled hole,
Widened by a will of prey,
But surely, as the evening now
      snuffs its light for night,
Shall the hands reach a plow,
Furrowing towards a lifting light?

Thus the shadow of love
Gathers hatred as untaught babe,
For the babe must be cuddled,
            admonished, and hugged
Before the vase is formed on lathe.

The vase formed and shaped on lath
Transports the cause
            to much quoted word
Whilst that hidden momented bird
Stays the cause of someone's word.

FAST FOOD

There were leftovers and no pie
            for my wee wife and I;
My son wouldn't eat,
My daughter wouldn't cry.
They went to McDonald's
To chew there by and by.

They say fast food
Is not good for the brood,
But piece for the stomach
And peace of the soul
Is better than nothing chewed.

When I was a kid,
Peanut butter stayed not long under the lid,
But the consumer does not kid—
When there's leftovers and no pie,
McDonald's has my bid;
Down to McDonald's we often fly.

THE TEETHING OF A FOE

Talk is like a mighty shadow
From the mouth of a foe,
Distorting the structured scene,
Gathering the nightwalker in tow
Onwards to feast of words,
Lengthening the nightly sentence,
Changing the math of life's true form,
Until the instruct of rising sun
Chases the shadow to other side.

WORDS WORTH CHOOSING

He who chooses gum chooses his words.
He who chews tobacco hates smoke.
A cigarette is an adult pacifier.
Drugs are for those afraid to be themselves.
Abortion is an outgrowth of hatred.
Contraceptives are for misers of love.
Divorce is a step never built by love;
Once built, the golden hammer turns to brass.
Love is a piece of heaven some would sacrilege.
Friends are nice until the f-r-i is lost.
Enemies are only envies.
Do you think dough is bread?
A problem is only a problem
Until the first step is taken.
Much may appear of a kiss until analyzed.
A jewelry box may appear so until opened.

BEST BEHOLDEN

It's open house all the time
Behind the star-quilted sky;
There're preparations for a feast
When a soul pulls the quilt, star shined,
O'er the twinkling, damning earthly lights.

Somewhere between the quilt and sheet,
The rose's rambling bloom
Shies the thorns of motored speech
With silvered clouds of ever perfume.
The aisleways are ever marked with angel smile,
Cherubim sing a seraphim symphony choir;
Ah, there's not noise and song
      and merriment always.

THE POWER OF ECOLOGY

I saw a field overgrown by rankest of weeds.
In a sea of seed wave to seed,
I saw masons and carpenters,
Plasterers and plumbers,
Electricians and roofers,
Holding their shape of build in mind;
Along came the cleaners shouting death not to a weed,
A foundation of durable stone
Soon rotted in place by changing of plans.

SERENITY

I live on an island
Where the waves kiss the shore,
Where once a friend,
A friend forevermore.

There's no need for pool,
There's no need for lock,
No need for dogs signaling
A breaking of the lock.

CHESTER'S HOME

There are those who say
Loneliness is an unkind word,
One heart in an uncaring crowd,
Lost in a theme park,
Waiting for an overdue plane.

My loneliness is a special sword
While sitting in a nursing home lobby,
Waiting for one I love
But doesn't seem to care.

That's okay;
It's a burden I've got to bear,
A torn heart I've got to share,
With the tiles and my trusty wheelchair.

Loneliness to me
Is going back to my room home
To sing my hymns all alone.

IMPATIENT IS THE ROAD

Soft Shoulders, so the road sign says,
Shaking me, the helmsman at wheel—
Truly my shoulders carry no one but me
        and my nagging bays;
Yes, and some other I may throw a deal.

My shoulder's not made for a cross;
Does it not say to my soul I'm its boss?
Yes, a rolling stone gathers no moss.
Why should I, my troubles on others tossed,
Let others cross the stream of cross,
Minding the way they're horsed.

Go on road and shake your sign,
You yellow diamond black of word;
Ne'er shall I seek your pine
Though 'tis once and e'er I've heard.

THE ANIMAL

Frogs hop and jump,
Insects fly and crawl;
Man beats his head
        against a wall,
So is his will, so is as pumped.

Frogs grow not their food,
Insects fly around their heads;
Frogs eat as is enough,
Man hoards which is not his stuff.

AT SHIFT'S END

Sound the bellows,
        let the day begin.
Sleep is for the fellows
Who would not a race to win.

Sound the bellows,
Churn the water's steam.
A melon only mellows
When the steam turns to stream.

Sound the bellows
        at end of workday's gain;
Though the mind be all callous,
Joy lives within the pain.

WORK CALL

Company's a-coming,
Get the place a-humming;
Don't walk around a-fumbling
Nor get overly a-chumming,
Just get the place a-rumbling.

The future may be a-crumbling,
You may find yourself a-tumbling;
Work's not for a-dumbling,
Show your pride,
        don't go off a-mumbling,
Show company work with pass
Makes a delicious dumpling.

SELF CARESSES

To the dunes we are led
  by the shifting winds of time,
Blowing from dune to dune
  a sand much fondled.

THE VALLEY STALKER

Justice is that space between
  the ear and eye;
What the ear cannot hear,
The eye dutifully sees.
What the eye cannot see,
The ear tunefully grasps.
What the ear nor eye cannot
  hear or see
Comes the meeting of the space
  in between to
The feel of the heard
The sight of the seen,
To meet on the shores of that
  space in between.

SONG TO THE LEAVES

When a bird sings,
The worm trembles on leaf;
When a worm eats,
The leaf joys to have given its
Part to the song of life.

When guns go boom
In the seasons of hunting time,
All nature creels in fright
Man's nonknowledge to
Life in a balanced scale.

When the spring's in bloom,
When summer lends a shade,
When fall begins a moan,
When winter salves a leisure time,
There's a symphony so quiet
Heard only by an ear attuned
To the song of bird,
The minioned meadow calls,
The strings of brook,
The wars of clouds,
Victoried by a leaf in fall,
All in song for the heart of man.

THE PAPERED FLICK

A director sits on his desk,
Pulls his mind in filmy net,
Thinks those thoughts
Common to thinking man.

Dreams, dreams, dreams,
Other thought dreams,
Plough his mind to will,
Sitting there in mental screams,
Gone to filmland's pool.

Perhaps, crossed his brow,
That jester of solemn mood,
He winks an eye
To human-viewing moods.

Sung his song
On pulsating lips
As eye-bothered mind
Flips away the papered flick.

HAPPY IS A CHRISTMAS SONG

Come on and sing Christmas song,
Light our hearts and chase the wrong.
Trim our tree with garlands long,
Happy is a Christmas song.

Now those lights are burning bright
On our tree on Christmas night.
There are gifts for all delight
Beneath the tree burning bright.

Heirlooms on a Christmas tree,
Though no money for you and me,
Just some things for us to see
How kinfolks love Christmas to be.

Now those lights are burning bright
On our tree on Christmas night.
There is love for all delight
Around the tree burning bright.

Come on and sing Christmas song,
Light our hearts and chase the wrong.
Trim our tree with garlands long,
Happy is a Christmas song.

THROW TITHES MY WAY

Priests bother me to no avail
With beggars' voice and rich clothes,
Drinking wine from common grail,
Sending words wherever blows
The flickering candle trail.

Wife minds me, duty to God:
Kitchen's filled to overflow,
Many clothes on trusty rod,
Savings in bank each day grow.

Wife sends me a lovely note:
Who's to break slavery's hoe
By building earth's house of God
And paying rent, just borrowed so,
'Til treasure's found after sod.

Wife means well in her small way:
Tithes another work of love
For God to have his same say
Much closer than from above.

OPEN GAITS

Flout your freedom
'Pon world at rest;
With works greet 'em
At their behest.

Languish those works
In others' yoke,
Roll your meaty hurts
In sorghum soaks.

Freedom's yoke springs
Cuttingly sharp
Through culture sings
Through broken harp.

Home freedom's bark
To friendly shores,
Better the spark
Than burning doors.

Anchor deeply
In hidden rust,
Tarnished meekly
In dawnings hushed.

POLLUTE WILL BE

Jets oozing gas in sky,
Clouds drinking jet trails
And urinating in our eye.

Cars in drunken oxide
Guzzle up eon's sunshine,
Burping gases plied
'Tween untuned whine.

Those things with half
The wheels as cars
Widen roads with laugh,
Chasing gas 'hind sissy bars.

Noisy-bladed, greedy maws
Cutting hair of earth
Strike our nostrils as claws
As blood screens gas, unworth.

Dairies with nicest of things,
Taurus and daisy,
Mults of thousand legs,
Suffer smells of waste
Content of give
That whitening fluid.

Millions, us humans,
Sit our pot and cry,
Listening surging waterfall,
Burdening our cries
Down dark tubes to potty house.

The fans of sun's hot shine
Each season's mourning tide
Makes big "nuddie" colony
As dress falls to feet.
Busy mites carry dress
To winds' widow's house.

Who that said
Pollute not now the law
Know us not;
The best learned through times,
The winds, rains, muds,
And sun that shines
Carries other pollutes
To other celestial realms.An Odious Ode
As an American, I pay my taxes,
I hold a daily job
And buy life's necessary waxes.
But many call me an uncomplaining slob
Because I'm of the minis instead of the maxis.

I read and ponder federal court decisions
And ink my mind in those legal cases
While I put off until tomorrow my derision,
Knowing there's a hitter on all the bases,
All because I'm of the minis instead of the maxis.

Congress, those two houses of politics,
Play their sandboxes against each other
While I'm at home trimming my wick,
And the darkness would have me smother
No matter how I devise and play my trick
All because I'm of the minis instead of the maxis.

Each two years I go to the polls
So ragged and torn by mental plunder;
I strike each name against my rolls,
But others tear my vote asunder
All because I'm of the minis instead of the maxis.

I've read my history from the national book
And wonder the lessons dancing undercover;
Still my vote is against that mouthy crook
Who laughs at Dad and smirks at Mother
On the job instead of on welfare's look
After the vote decides his druthers,
All because I'm of the minis instead of the maxis.

I'm denied a raise or so
With all that corporation taxes' clutter;
My nation steals from my heart its glow
With its old engine about to sputter,
Laden so heavily with taxes' snow,
All because I'm of the minis instead of the maxis.

Millions are given to presidential candidates
        All aglow with buffoonery's say,
But only one to the nation relates,
Speaking of the poor and a brighter day;
One would think this a nation of reprobates,
All because I'm of the minis instead of the maxis.

When I reach that golden city on the hill
After tolls and trolls wear my heart thin,
I've no pittance to seed my nation's drill
Except a weapon in arm and a drunkard's grin;
Now I'm of the maxis instead of the minis.

FIRE IN THE WOODS

There's in my soul God's good miracle!
He lives in me! Now that's a miracle!
He works through me a mighty miracle!
He's given all! I'm his miracle!

He walks on this earth so in love with me!
He watches over the winds in my tree!
He sends his spirit! My bonds are so free.
Oh, he has worked a miracle in me!

I'm upon his road! His glory shines!
In my soul, there a treasure he finds!
I'm in his book that eternity binds!
He gives to me a crown! His glory shines!

Oh, come you peoples from fare and wide,
Beneath his wings he will surely all hide
You from the wiles of death and will's cruel tide;
And with love, faith, and hope, his fields are wide!

I have suffered long for my love of him,
But that suffering is joy to the brim
For there is no pain when love is the trim
Of a life walking its way to him!

There's in my soul God's good miracle!
He lives in me! Now that's a miracle!
He works through me a mighty miracle!
He's given all! I'm his miracle!

AND CREATOR MUST CREATE

Spin off a planet and a comet's light,
Finger of God touches distances;
Stars are counted twinkling at night,
Angels in song with litanies.
Gardens have grown to life as called,
And man is joyed in God's own life,
Eternal souled in flesh so walled,
To care his home with loving wife.
Hope and will and a bright star's ride,
Freedom's on path in darkest space
Candled with love and fire's confide
Of faith that rooms with highest grace.
Endeavors with a tinge of fate
To build his castle's fortress wall,
Only to lay in grave's dark wait—
Only to rise again when God does call.

THIS THING CALLED SPIRIT

We search the clouds above
and find a promise of rain in season.
  We look at the face of the moon
and ponder the restlessness of the stars.
  We hoe our garden in spring
and trust nature's laws for dutiful mercy.
  We walk our daily paths in fun or work
and know the day could have been better.
  We know the face of a friend
as the enemy thirsts for friendship.
  We have our qualms and quiet example
and think ours the worst or better.
  We train our lives and ofted forget our soul
and wonder our nondeveloping world.
  We know there's a source and course for all
at the beck of this thing we call Spirit.
  We know there's a Spirit issued from God
and numb our hands stuffed close in pocket.
  This thing we call Spirit
depends upon us to spin the world,
to call the clouds and face the moon,
to hoe our garden and walk our paths,
to have as friends our former enemies
if they have tried to gladden our soul
for in this we have calmed our soul
in the touch of this thing called Spirit.

SHIBBOLETHS 'ROUND ME PLAY

Go limpid by the bedside
Of life's sweet-bitter dish,
There's others chaffing the good
Under some smelly garbage lid.

Go limpid by the bedside
Of society's mooding gone ways,
Smothered in darkened gravy
For want of peer's say.

Go limpid by the bedside
Of familial harping songs,
Craving, craving indeed,
For the birds of love's rose.

Go limpid by the bedside
Of one's sane, rehearsed time,
Muddled by nerves' sharp tone,
Speaking limpidly,
"What's the use?"

Go limpid by the bedside
Of history's true meat
Gone, gone, the familial home,
Crying, crying in dream,
Of what's the use.

FAIRLY DONE

Meet you at the fair,
Meet you in the way;
Noisy booths of curious flair
Break once-full pocket while play.

Meet you at the fair,
At tedious works of ware,
Where worst-wrought work
Sparks judges' mental quirk;
Only haps at the fair.

Meet you at the fair,
In nose tingling for shut,
Round fly-dappled, sweet booth.

Meet you at the fair.
Meet you in the air.
Meet you in the way.
Meet you at the ware.
Meet you in the free.
Just meet me everywhere.

CHALLENGE OF LIFE

Woke up this morning,
Eyes bathed in pain,
Tongue thick as cubes of ice,
Mouth wishing bath in sea,
Belly not in feel of nice,
Just for juice of grain.

Morning blues sing so perf,
Nary more I'll touch the stuff
And find myself a faithful serf
Just for juice of grain.

Cursed my wife at breakfast time
For lateness of coffee and rind;
Saw myself in silly pants
Just for juice of grain.

Changed my habit,
Changed my speech,
Changed my love
For juice of grain.

IMPEDED

E'er watched the grasses grow
In diverse height and spread
None with same splendored glow
Kinds with different head?
Their toes of varied depth
All to earth kissed in wed
As all seasons' wind blow
Their secrets of God kept.

Come the bee in solace
Danced his high wedding song,
Stayed his wee time as pressed
Fore nature called him wrong;
Whence we find selves blest,
Helping in sorrows long.

WHERE THE STREET CHILDREN LAY

A young face reflecting from pond of a soul disturbed
Beneath a shivered, cold snow drifted, crackling hell's scene.
Mother Love abandons refuge den, once downy herbed.
Father's teach, now an axe in back, empty bag of bean.

A young face so puzzling, jigsaw haven lent to hell.
Friends forsake friendship, untie not its given box.
Home once heaven, now a fire gone out, denizens yell.
Rats gnaw at moldy cheese. The hour has stilled all the clocks.

A young face pawing frown fades last soft face of love's rain.
The street, a refuge yearning, heaven's lost. Hell's burning.
The grass of wit, nobly left, on the face of clown's pain.
Tearful eyes, expression rent. Milk of life not churning.

A young face bleeding. Nature's retreat house receding.
Problems mount. Love's vestige has no recount. Acid smile.
Ghosts infest. Unlighted house screams. Love's not releasing.
Gone the thistle bloom. Tare weighs the road. Heavy is the mile.

A young face seen, reflections of society's screen:
Broken web, moth encased, and spidery veil so undated.
Hurt in soul, gone love's scold. Hate offers rust so unclean,
Where the street children lay, cast by a love not imbued.

A young face seen. Life reflects of society's screen:
Broken web. Moth encased. Spidery veil so recluse.
Hurt in soul. Gone love's scold. Hate offers rust so unclean,
Where the street children lay, cast by unlove on the loose.

JUBILEE

One gen brings freedom,
Next gen brings war;
Live today,
Let the morrow
Be worth dying for.

Ring out your bells,
In concert sing your song;
Char your fatted beasts,
Eat sweet-veined flesh.

Converse with assembly
In windy atmos' mood.
Taste the sugared crusts,
Drink fermented seed.

Taint sociable,
A wallflowered mode.
(There's walls of home
To flaunt mental brood.)
So drink the fermented seed.

Sing your chorus of freedom
In untutored tune.
Thank your God in earthy word
That all lies not in ruin.

Bring guitars to woodwind's call,
Make a joyous noise
In concert, each and all.
Is not the morrow's fare
Heard in lustful soothe?
Eat, drink, and be merry,
Tackle the morrow's snare.

The morrow shall surely come
As day draws its shade,
Betoken of next glorious sunburst.
Each eye in skyward tilt
Sees man-made lights
Crackling and thundering,
Enchanting the festive air,
Branding each soul
In country's freedom flair.

O'er the whole wide world,
Some part has its cankerous sore;
Be joyful that the morrow
Shall bind those wounds in lore.

Sound your crashing cymbals
In inattentive ear.
Finger the trembling flute
On the waning minds of men.

Pluck the violins' strings
And quicken its dusty bow;
Tell all in jubilee
There're fields yet to mow,
Songs yet to sing
With words of future tune.
There're birds in the forest
Yet to be heard and seen.

Feast the eye,
Fill the belly,
Ingratiate the soul
In freedom's great mixing bowl.

'Tis for the babes,
'Tis for the old;
So ring out your bells,
In concert, sing your soul.

IN MY GARDEN JUNGLE

Poor public worker in eight-houred grub
Spades his garden for victory place
As twilight's finger on eve rub,
Thinking he's up to gardening pace.

Spring's all well in cool time
As hypocrites under blanket lay
Waiting the sun in hotter climb
Fore their faces they bluntly display.

Pigweed, what your purpose be,
Offspringing me with dire misery,
Hoeing you down fore grown into a tree?
Sundry selfish weed you be,
Smothering my garden's cabbage, wee.

Purslane, purslane, pretty, greening weed,
Too lazy for known of height,
Too weak for backache strain impede,
Too blind for need of light,
Just rambling on foraging ground,
Shading other toes in wait of crown
Though you make good eating pound.

Why spread your arms for all to see,
You poorest of weeds in sight of man?
In rags your children romp in melee,
Thinking poor gets pennies in pan.
You adults in mischief rags
Cry many tears of dust
Collected in human eyeing bags.

Jim's son's weed in need of bath
Blows his bugles all day long
But begging night moth's wrath
Come to dance in his song.
With bugles encased by night's sleep,
Jim's son husband's spiny toy
For pretty marbles in box of keep;
He's playing secrets of deadly deploy.

Poor public worker in eight-houred clock
Grows his grub to muscles weep,
Looking forlorn to growing flock.
He spurts out wisdom for all's keep:
See one's wife to garden crop
Fore sporting work rags off to work.
She's no work after mop.
She's the one my spirits perk.

BY BREAD ALONE

Saw a fatso
Sitting in booth,
Minding own business,
Eating sweets and cream,
Pleasing sweet tooth.

Saw a skinny one
Sitting beside,
Minding own business,
Eating bran and meat
Fatso could not abide.

Fatso wo-man,
Skinny hu-man,
Nature's way
Of balanced flesh.

Fatso wo-man
Walks for job in vain,
Hearing future boss
Fire words in rebuke,
"Why'd you come
All dressed in fat?"

Skinny hu-man
With no flesh to lose
Works, works as work demand,
Punishing self
In fatso's staid.

COLOR

Are we to push the sun aside
Since yellow we no longer can abide?
Are we to clear all forests green
Since we consider it of sickly sheen?
Are we to cover the earth's brown
If it reminds us of some humans around?
Are we to burn nature's oils of light
If we like not the black of night?
Are we to trample the flag's many stripes
Because of red we have our gripes?
Do put on reason's warm touching glow,
Show the less-learned
Which direction the wind should blow.
Cower not in the coward's cloak of slight;
Disease needs weaklings
To become a blight.

FIRE IN YON CAMPSITE

With head bowed in friendship's press,
I spin my web encircled within
Friendship's new moon,
Orbiting 'round warm stars in spark,
Twinkling, enlightened, enthroned
'Pon essayed bliss.

Twinkle my stars
In heaven's clear sea;
Burn 'til words' fathomed ship
Burst its doors in watery spurn.
Heap tirades of nerves enjoy
On this friendship's bright flame.

THE LASTING EMBRACE

Shushed in while, gypsy's mash
Brightens yawning hour;
I cast heather's sweet bane
O'er my spun web, enflamed,
Enflamed, indeed enflamed,
To smiles' sauntering, wispy sprite
E'er watchful to coals' ebbing sight,
Whitened once and only
In hypnotic, trancing plane.
Embers die but once,
My friendship and love
Dies heartily, slowly,
In hearts my embers touch.

'TWAS EXPLAINED TO ME

Streams trickle in this heart,
Gathering love's waters,
Broadening e'er so wide;
As to the river of your love,
It rushes in quickening abide.

This stream that trickles in my heart
Fills in days of arrow sped
In path towards my heart,
Maddeningly plowing the roots
From love's ofttimes sleeping tree.

Waters of love winding 'round
Your tree of love,
E'er in wanton respite
To conquer the spirit of love;
As strongly, daily it grows
To newly born,
More lofty greening heights.

Come drop your leaf of love
In my sudden-gushing stream.
Come wade the feet of love
In my refreshing, cool waters of stream.
Come, I'm but a tributary
Emptying self
To your river of love.

Come, rain your tears,
Fill my stream.
Come, smile my waters
Sincere and clean.
Come, swim my length,
Wade my breadth;
I'm but the half of love.

APATHY QUICKENED

Little worm in your hole,
Do you feel winter's cold?
Summer's hot,
And spring's balm.
Are you wrapped in song,
Secure in dusty walls?

Little worm in hole,
Do you hear
Thunder of feet,
Chirp of bird,
Plows a-crashing,
Grit blocking your door?

Little worm in hole,
Do you understand:
Rain flooding floor,
Mold eating store
Of workload panned?
Quiet antennae,
'Tho not busy in shade,
Cogs whirr 'neath?

Little worm in hole,
Do you oft regret
Many legs too weak,
Greedy mouth
In others' worked stew,
Many-faceted eye,
For simple brain,
Fainting oft in heighted rye?

Little worm in hole,
Why glutton food?
I see you ashamed
In shame's mire.
Why spin your cocoon
Of unmatched gossamer?
I see you in change;
Change to prettier,
More worthy pacer
For nature's loveways.

BUSING ROW

Hit him o'er the head,
He, reasoner,
Stripping human traits.

Hit him o'er the head,
The stylused one,
Grieving pen in law.

Hit him o'er the head,
I say,
Hit him o'er the head.

Hit him o'er the head,
Dark reasoner,
Grieving children's bones.

Grieving children's bones
Far away from homes,
Statured in busing's law.

Did you hear my plea?
Hit him o'er the head.
Hit him o'er the head.

THE PETALLED BLADE

If one cannot say
      or express
Life's different and varied
      emotions,
Whether they be joyous,
      sad, or empathetic,
With flowers of vase,
Then, 'tis then
Life had indeed lost its touch
      with reality.

No other object on earth
Can bring such a song
      without words,
Singing, shouting, praying,
And smiling the receiver's
        heart
Than the singular beauty
Of a petalled stalk of grass.

At birth
      the enraptured emotions
To love's fitting song
Cannot—no, cannot—
        be expressed,
Fully expressed, except
Through a swaddling cloth
Lovingly laid upon
      love's table
In a vase of purest white.

THE RANK OF BATTLE

The flowing, ofttimes eccentric scenes bubbling forth from the intermingled paths of growing up unto death's inevitable greet cannot be fittingly expressed except through a bladed, color-splotched vase of petaled grass.
If mankind is to fathom love, which has no filling word;
Joy, which has no tongue; grief, which oftentimes has no tears, mankind must look to the humbleness of nature, saying all.

If there be anyone who lives
          and makes not waves against religion,
They're in the business of growing pines
Instead of oaks of dominion.

When the Flossys come and shake their ships,
To men studying their trusty oars,
Something's got to give, my child,
Either the waves or the sanding shores.

While the wars of good and evil
Shake a life of unloosened hold,
There be thousands following the wake,
Gathering wrecks once strong and bold.

The young are taught to the sage's tell,
But youth cares not its reason;
There's more to writ in the teacup's smell
Than love be man's highest treason.

In the harbor, there'll be its waste,
There'll be the skunks and rats of evil,
Wrestling in the winding road to haste.
There'll be always the youth to weasel
Adulterating modes from the paste.

Until day and night grow confused
        and the moon bests in battle the sun,
The clock of mind shall ever be amused
With the toy of wisdom's fun.

If there be anyone who lives
        and makes those waves for religion,
Their business of growing pines
Shall down those oaks of dominion.

FLY TIME

A fly will often see its worm.
A fly sometimes makes one squirm.
A fly will open its wings
      at unexpected times.
A fly has its quoted rhymes.
If it weren't for a fly,
      waters would stale,
So the next time you sight a fly,
Be thankful for a zipper
      colloquially called a fly.

THE AGEING WILLOW

By the pond of reflection
ages are told in moving glass,
rippled by the wind,
misted by a passing sun
with everlasting shimmered glimmer,
repetitious to a mourning moon,
seeing, drinking roots of dreams,
feeding leaflets clinging to breasts
until the light of day
suns its warmth to life,
drinking, feeling reminisces
as a struggled prisoner, free.

ON THE LEVEE

Fishing on the jetty
      with eyes glued to spray,
Just I and my sweet Betty
      caught no fish today.
We sailed the seas and sunny skies,
We kissed the stars and slept the sun,
We listened to jetty bird cries
      until our fishing was quite done.
Still we haven't caught no fish
      since love is a lovely dish.

LITTLE TOO MUCH

I'm a little too young
and a little too old
to play my games of chess or gun.
I'm a little too young
and a little too old
to do my thing or spend my gold.
I'm a little too young
and a little too old
to speak my will or life that's sprung.
I'm a little too young
and a little too old
to dream my dream or set my goal.
I'm a little too young
and a little too old
to see with eyes or watch my tongue.
There's nothing for me
but to take myself and change
the world with what's left there.

THE RICHEST MAN

Is he who owns the universe, not
with hands of gold or power,
neither by authority's tongue,
but with regrets and remorse
        for the powerless
gone a chasing freedom's rainbows
in adversity's sure gone, hopes
for victory's rot of future will?
Thus it is in the dream of riches
that the power of the powerless
rises and falls all dominions,
giving wealth to him who owns
        the universe
found in the cry of a child.

TENTS OF LIFE

Copulation,
Annunciation,
Incarnation,
Experimentation,
Exasperation,
Rationalization,
Rejuvenation,
Expiration,
Resurrection
In another's dream.

ROADSIDE ADS

The sea licking
at the shoulder of a coastal highway.
Seagulls
greased to death in an oil slick.
A cigarette
charcoaling scenic forests.
Price supports
rotting in mountains of famine food.
Politics
making backyard arsenals.
Nations
gossiping in gibberish.
Religion
parting the oceans with storms.
People
at war within
while maggots fail to metamorphose
and roadside ads sink behind
the underbrush.

THE COWARDS OF AIR

Hijackers hide themselves in flights
  And soar upon the windy heights
With helpless hostages in air
  And soar upon the windy heights.

Thinking will as done is as come,
  Giving pride to cowards with none;
Hijackers hide themselves in flights
  And soar upon the windy heights.

Hijackers hide themselves in flights
  And soar upon the windy heights,
Like vultures eating carrion,
  And soar upon the windy heights,
With their bones denied of heart,
  Bleeding of soul in dark of hell.

Hijackers hide themselves in flights.

THE PREVAILING WAY

A skull upon the sand lay
Bleached by salt, sun, and tide;
Listen closely to its bay
Shouting 'pon atoms plied
'Tween sand, water, and tide at play.

Soulful, screaming, beckoning,
Abode of eyes no more
Search the flight of gull on wing
In mind of good nesting door,
Who, in quick and fitful flay of tutored sing,
Shies these holes of eye no more.

Great hinged jaw froze in shouting
One last eternal syllable
Plied in barrowed energy,
Pushed on shore's hidden road,
Swept invisible between sand and space.

Sand crabs in ever fiddled play
Climb that whited picket fence
That once hid in secret under fleshy clay
As mother sea scrubs in recompense
Her children caught behind the picket way.

Dull those sounds, you pounded sand,
Cymbal led each second o'er
By crashing, crushing, maddened waves
In known of deafened ears of skull.
Those maddened waves in welcoming voice,
To have their tales of sob,
Told to skull in vibrations' ring.

In solitudinous quiet,
The hermit of once habited frame
Forsakes his crowed cabin
For this many-doored and whited mansion,
Wasting on shore's covering sand.

Smile again, you laughing, seeing, hearing bone;
The hermit comes on speed
For you his home on loan,
You the visitor to this shore,
In wait of tides' high time.

See, you eyes out of sight,
Hear, you ears without clap;
Smell, you nose, the quiet of night,
Close, you jaws, in painting flap
As waves and sea and sun and moon
Wink between the towing currents
To this skull stalking a hermit's trail.
Walking the hermit's way,
The way of prevail.

A NECKLACE HE GAVE

Wear a necklace 'round your neck,
Carrying mini two-beams
Crocheted in gold-silvered lace.

My love's off yon in my other heart,
Picking violets for my perfume
As I make rhubarb sweet-spicy tarts
With my love's necklace chasing my gloom.

Wear a necklace 'round your neck,
Carrying mini two-beams
Crocheted in gold-silvered lace.

Hi-lo, soft wand in bye hovered start,
Ticking sigh-o-lets from my presume;
Do you have really lots special darts,
Daring love's greening worship, free doom?

Wear a necklace 'round your neck,
Carrying mini two-beams
Crocheted in gold-silvered lace.

Cry love oft wrong when my other heart's
Sticking by for frets from my sursums;
'Tho I make rubble greet speaky parts,
Daring love's necklace sharing my room.

Wear a necklace 'round your neck,
Carrying mini two-beams
Crocheted in gold-silvered lace.

Grown crazed in love for my other heart,
Drying bit by bit for me and groom,
As I make pretty sweet-spicy tears
Dance down love's necklace,
Gracing while chasing my gloom.

Wear a necklace 'round your neck,
Carrying mini two-beams
Crocheted in gold-silvered lace.

Great nuptial hour come none too soon;
My fingers strum great chain on neck.
I pick my violets in mental corsageing tune
As my love throws a soothing fleck.

Wear a necklace 'round your neck,
Carrying mini two-beams
Crocheted in gold-silvered lace.

I wear his necklace 'round my neck,
Carrying his love while away;
He's crocheted in gold-silvered lace.

TEARS BY THE LIGHTHOUSE

To the mansions of history's lore,
All are called to wave, to mourn,
      to cry, to joy,
With the gentle lead of a common touch
When all's in all, not all in one,
Pulled by the gentle lead
      of a nation's president.

Bon Secour to the bon voyage,
Bonjour to the Bon Secour.
Midnight tows another bonjour,
Reason tows every Bon Secour
When a president has that common touch
In the Bon Secour of the common man.

Many there are reaching for the stars,
Waking in a reflected sea;
Few there are called to rule,
Greatly wisdomed, reasoned miniscule,
Until the eyes are lifted
From the changing sanding bars,
Twinkling a joy gone waking in soul.

Bon Secour to the bon voyage,
Bonjour to the Bon Secour;
Day has dawned
          upon the reflected sea,
Truth is seen upon the frothy wake.

Truth is seen beyond the frothy wake,
A president rules in the Bon Secour
          of the common man.
By the gentleness of a common touch,
All lie gutted to the newborn sun
As citizens wave in the misty sea
Down by the shore of Bon Secour
Blown by the winds of a president.

To the mansions of history's lore,
          all are called
To wave, to mourn, to cry, to joy,
Down by the lighthouse of gentle lead,
Where tears roll out to the sea beyond,
Pulled, tossed, and returned
To the lighthouse beam of a president.

TURBULENCE

Turbulence wakes this body of mine,
Grazing in pastures, otherwheres,
My course having set life's goal
In thunderings and boisterousness.

I walk mine path side everglades,
Even to highest mountaintop,
In search mine vacant place,
Where presence of God may be heard.

I entered the fierce, galling wind
In hopes his anger be heard,
But he was not there.

I ran along the earthquake's rim;
I many times shook to ground
As my God I wished to hear;
But he was not there.

I cringed in hearing of fire's wrath,
Minding not its acrid breath,
Just longing for that voice of God;
But he was not there.

I too long in looking at the fire,
Forgot the fire encircling me,
As a voice in desperation cried,
"Over here, over here, please help me."

'Tho I in danger's seat did run
To voice of brother's cry.
'Tis then, 'tis then, I heard,
I heard that soft whisper
I'd been searching for.

Then, oh then, in prayer lifted high,
In silenced lips I praised
The spirit of Mighty One
For call of me to this place
In soft whispering to soul,
The louder, louder by far,
Than winds and earthquakes
And crackling brightest fires.

NIGHTMARES AND STALE HORSES

Since you've run from me into your oceans alone,
Nightmares and stale horses
Run pastures from dawn to dawn, with poison's atone,
Galloping up to a face. Turning, it's not you.
Nightmares and stale horses
Paw the ground. Eat nervously. Grass drinking not dew.
Morn pardons not night cast shadows in prison break.
Birds oddly quiet their song for solitude's sake.
Hooves beat daily pounded paths. Dust inebriates
Nightmares and stale horses
That cloud of inextricableness obdurate,
Which, even the evening honeysuckle scent,
Stales the lingered air. I listen for your repent.
Nightmares and stale horses
Eye my obliquity, my immoral conduct
Of looking, listening for your return abrupt.
Oh, if my literacy could obliterate feel,
I'd trade my nightmares and stale horses for death's steel.

SMOKE ON FIRE

We forget about our genes
      and blame all on outward scenes.
We cry against genetics
      and birth our own aesthetics.
Why worry of cigarettes?
      There're more worthy niggard frets.

Which is worse, cigarettes, broken nerves?
Each has problem with the one it serves.
If cigarettes are quite known to kill,
      doesn't abortion the same pot fill?

Government versus morals it is,
      protecting us from an unknown fizz.
If I wish to do, my problem is,
      I can't escape mine, thine, or God's biz.

The trouble with us grown-ups,
      we all have problems with our hiccups.
We all do not want to ever die
      but ever reach for death's pie in sky.

If we do live through all the forests,
      taste the good, the bad, and the sorriest,
How are we to say how death began
      when pollution surrounds everyone?

RICHMOND ON THE JAMES

On to Richmond,
The place of rich, jealous mud,
Swirled o'er the rapids
By James round the hills,
Round the gambling hill—
The Oregon hill—
Where rests the rugged and silent:
The full-ton hill
Laced with tracks.
Three great hills
All in seething ooze
Cry the contested battle:
I'll kill ole James
While four dressing hills
Rest in quiet of fear.

On to Richmond,
The city of seven hills,
Dwarfed by high capitol one
Guarded on that hill
By equestrian general, nigh.

On to Richmond
To see ancient avenue
Sequined by greening sepulchered
Watchmen of the past,
Smiling yet staunchly in path,
The path of Monument Row.

On to Richmond
To buy me a fan
Held by Monroe's hand,
Beringed in jewels fair:
There's mosque stone
For fancy party fair.
There's cathedral stone
For formal wear.
There's Jefferson stone
Lost in boudoir chair.
There's Mecca Cevite stone
To wear in bed upstairs
While wounds heal, all alone.
There's Mansion stone
To flirt the eye, all aglare.
There's rupee Inca stone
For classes everywhere.
I've a stone for everyplace
That shines in freedom's fair.

On to Richmond,
Fair city seat,
To see my horseman of the street,
To see the broad fairway
Noisy by the hawkers' beat
Neath old stone castle's feet.

On to Richmond,
Richmond on the James,
To hear fair bells
Rung to dogwood bud,
Blooming on the lawn
That bleeds Byrd's song.

On to Richmond,
My road leads me 'long
The lanes of histories homes
Long stood by freeman's cry:
I build my house
Amongst the people
Not in some fortress wall.

On to Richmond,
Jewel pot of melting fame.
On to Richmond
If your freedom flame
Dies low to embers.

On to Richmond,
To Richmond go,
Have your dreams
Pulled to humanity's prow,
Helmed by Virginia's sons,
Waking ancient deeds,
Storming the seven hills,
Guarding my fair city
Called the jewel pot
Of melting fame
'Round the river James.

PILES STRUCK THE GLASS

How 'twas said
Watergate,
The beginning
This nation's ruinous fate,
Inframed with many faces,
Glowering as coals, red.

Why 'tis we live each day,
Faking ego's pedestal,
'Membering not the day
Of yesterday:
It too sketched
In much-charred coals
Wanton for the artist's brush.

The price too dear
As on a palette lay
Flushed in strokes bold,
These gains of illegal tear.

Must we drive our piles
Close to looking glass
As in staggering afterthought
We strike our image
Impaled in glass?

THE CURIOSITY SHOP

Trends in reversals' maws
Held fast by habits' throes
Grapples its thread sheet
As tearing vein from flesh.

This symbol of fashioned heat
Hung on bodies crazed
Breaks the bookie's back
As brokers be the name
For same old tricks.

A penny a bag
In bag unseen,
This the curiosity shop
Stinging minds' mental flaw
Enchained by nonreversals' maws.

UN AND DE

What could I do
As upon my path I walk,
Seeing shadows of the past,
Stagnant pools in rutted talk?

What could I do
For the foraging millions bread
But turn my eye,
Shake this body's head,
Then on my path proudly walk?

What could I do
In the noisy chambers of man,
Like as waves upon the sand,
Tangled in twisted,
Garbled sounds?

What could I do
But walk my path,
Minding my way,
Just giving a laugh—
Critic of a bad play?

What could I do
But echo the refrain
Of some loud voice
That turned me on
My path once again?

What could I do
But ride some lonesome train
Bedecked with heads
Of hairy chins gone grey
Neath its unshorn plain,
Betoken of a silent majority's blain?

What could I do
But walk my path again
In silent remorse of rectitude?
'Twas I who hast not lain
Betwixt the silent beatitudes,
Only walked my path once again.

UNSTEADY

In the room where rests my bed,
Proudly stands many drawered chest,
Making nightstand much afraid,
Standing off with no request.

Walls donned in bright-painted dress
Guard this room's many drawered chest,
Whose shaved head gleams in polish,
Adorned with trinkets as bows
Seemingly hover in thin air.

Neath balded head's brim-capped edge,
Two large eyes open and shut,
Baring many motes and beams
While accusing my nightstand
Of moving closer to bed.

My nightstand cries with an eye
In presence of bald head brute
Standing so awkward astute,
"I'm the holder of light and time,
You the hider of body's dress."

BRINKY BANKS

Go us to the brink
Of life's shallow pool,
Drink us of waters never touched by hands,
Shapened not by carnal moods.

Go we to the brink
Of stillen waters shaked
By our small pebbles
Thrown at distance length,
Pitched from quaked shadows.

Go we to the brink
Lain in silted thought,
Mourned by anxious
Limbs, nimbled by nerves
Don't care after draught.

Go we to the brink
Of daily grown bides,
Watch we nature's qualms
Shook in man's pied
Worker, sulken, no alarms.

Go we to the brink
In pleasures' bright attire,
Sit we 'mongst scoundrels
Made 'pon our pennied moats.
'Tis we looked in our bier.

Go we to the brink
Worked frothy in wake
By our borrowed craft
Stirred in automation,
No helmsman baying cry.

Go we to the brink
Of life's shallow pool,
Gaze we 'pon an image
So marvelous imbued;
Yet we each day's fool.

Go we to the brink,
List we echoing sounds,
Moods, shadowed thoughts
Pied in covering attire
As craft listlessly wanes.

Go we to the brink,
Drink deep in life's draught;
Heed sounding conscience
Fore many pebbles thrown
Stir our mix, all taciturn.

NETTLED FLESH

Call me fore crack of dawn
Just to let chickens
Scratch up lawn.

Crack the whip o'er my head;
Call me names
But not Uncle Jed.

Set me at kitchen table;
Feed me vittles,
Which I can't label.

I tread the row
'Til twilight dim,
Spading weeds with a hoe.

Send me home to wife and kids,
Tell me of next day's chore;
Weight my mind to sleeping skids.

Teach my kids in shanty house
Way from whiteys
Afraid of catching louse.

Teach me of kingdomed God
Of love and golden rule,
Keep me well fed and shod.
Sing me hymns 'pon phantom horse,
Kick my ribs,
And show me who's boss.

Restrict your house with pricing rods;
I'm not human
To jive your weighty pods.

Elect your men in riches' pool,
Break my back,
And lay me a welfare's fool.

I hang my flag o'er door someday,
Whisper to self,
"O God, is this the way?"

Bury me in segregated hole,
Thank me not
For songs and labor told.

THE COMMON TOUCH

O lovely, isn't it,
When skies are blue
And feet get wet
With morning dew?
Lovely, isn't it?

Lovely, isn't it,
When lazy bones
Spread o'er the shade
Watched some frog
In his lily pad chair?
Lovely, isn't it?

Lovely, isn't it,
To sip thy juleps minted green
And sit in nature's calm,
Welcoming sway,
Sends her moth
To sip thy windward way?
Lovely, isn't it?

A STAR IN BATTLED BLOOD

Remember the Alamo
As taught in schooling books:
How the general
Washed his hands in tide,
Slowly ebbing battle's crust
To stronger nation's bide.

Look o'er those pages
Writ in clotted black blood.
See beneath the soldier's cap
Strength embroiled in scud.

See the great arched portal,
Lonely but to sky it reached,
Catching one star lonely
Cloven to manly pride.

Thank the star in battled blood
The watchman of this nation's crest;
'Tis not oft, one star lonely
Takes the creel for a nation's fest.

One star lonely
Rippling und portal's shade,
Reckons to free men only
Rest not at my feet
Till all in freedom's battle
Wipes and hangs the blade.

Remember the Alamo
Not taught in schooling books:
A battle's not battle
With only one side.

Look me in the distance,
Ponder enemy died;
We only on one side once
'Til battle dims our pride.

MY DREAM

Oh, for the good ole days
In beauty, wine, and song:
Beauty unto the face lays
Workings into the other parts.

Frills in lace,
Dainty shrouds to gladden hearts
Of suitors fine redress,
Dampened not in remorse.

Oh, for the good ole days,
In search of a woman's heart—
Mental task indeed
That gladdened the start
Of romance plucking the weed.

Oh, for the good ole days,
Flesh bared not
'Til the bells of vows
Changed two as one.

Gossamer, gingham, and lace
Dressed in hide
That surging feel left undone:
Suitor's heights in mental paint
Must touch the final brush
Fore body's flesh unveiled.
How else 'tis love should grow
'Cept in heart's felt warmth
Fore fleshy shock
Stunts, taints, and cracks
This fragile bowl of heart?

Oh, for the good ole days,
Sweet, bitter moments of wine:
Memory's lane washed bare
For want of skinny scene.

Gossamer, lace, silk, and brac;
Delicate smell from
Hot, chafing dish
Quickens the heart's felt warmth.

One longing
For the chastity
Of former
Days' courtship.

COLOR

Are we to push the sun aside
Since yellow we no longer can abide?

Are we to clear all forests, green,
Since we consider it of sickly sheen?

Are we to cover the earth's brown
If it reminds of some humans around?

Are we to burn nature's oils of light
If we like not the black of night?

Are we to trample the flag's many stripes
Because of red we have our gripes?

If answer cannot ready be,
Put on reason's warm touching glow,
Show the less learned
Which direction the wind should blow.

Cower not in the coward's cloak of slight;
Disease needs weaklings to become a blight.

Show your color in noonday sun.
Show your color in dark of night.
Show your color to barking gun.
Show your color when out of sight.

THISTLE DOWN

Ablaze in joy awhile,
Athwarth caught in court's aisle,
Revengeful nettles
Tear at necklaced lifestyle:
Good Book and choir soon forgot
As joys and vows
In windy atmosphere
Securely covers love
With wispy tauntings' hate.
Sagacious whispers of marriage bed
Feed greedy public jaws,
Whose unwritten law
Decoys a spiritual lead,
Marooned in sin flaw.

How doth flirts change love so quick?
Wonder if there were love at all,
Extinguishing flame with a flick
That shook the wand to its fall.

Oh, rancid, crackling-natured man,
In shadows seeks a flick,
Where fires extinguish love's fair fan,
Demeaning my love's image
By thinking love's a trick,
Leaving thistle blooms to self
And I waiting the thistle down.

NEVER WAVE GOOD-BYE

There is . . .
Bell in belfry,
Love infests the heart,
Choir in sweetened memory,
Friends enchanting air,
Twain 'pon altar's tier,
Eyes as pools of bliss,
Lips in words-fair hallow,
Ears bearing not their code,
Ring 'pon pillow lies,
Hand entwined in script,
Nerves pumped by bellows
Wait the wanted phrase,
Teeth chattery as said I do,
Rice freckling the scene,
Feet stumped
By love's light load,
Disdaining stones great height;
Despiteful doors,
The loathsome need;
Unhurried love's great flight,
Reposing in joy's last great scene
As friends notice ply;
Resentful seas of hands
Quiver the wave good-bye
To travelers on waves, high,
Chanting love song,
Never, never wave good-bye.

LONELY

Hang my body
In Hellman's canyon,
Drown my bones
In pity's chasm;
Bark ye coyote's
In askance bay,
'Tis but me
Waning in spasm.

Worms may hole my body
In Hellman's canyon,
Fish may pick my bones
In pity's chasm,
Coyotes may bark
Me lonely tune,
'Tis but me
Gone, gone
This way too soon.

O'ERCLOUDED

The storms of life
Are but duty past
That compunction
Lathes its part;
We must duly
Fit our piece
If only to soil
Our cloth
In lacquered
Masterpiece
'Haps no one
Would have but you.

The storms of life
Clouded o'er much,
Shakes in the drumming
Of thunders' peal
Though in wait
For lightning struck
Fore commencing
Its rains of worth.

The storms of life,
Ever hovering,
Ne'er past
By our fresh
And warm breastworks
'Tho mostly weaned,
Desirious of suck
Remain near
To our lightnings,
Thunders, and squalls,
Knowing each storm's center
Passes quickly fore done.

STREAKING BORN

I was to streaking born
In Eden's animal paths,
I was to streaking born
Void of eyeing laughs.

In the shadow of Adam
We shed our stolen cloths,
Worn snugly to flesh,
Yet mind sweeps our lofts
Of clothing balmed in mesh.

See our tainted thoughts
Taken from marriage bed,
Thrown to damper's draughts,
Picked by dickering head,
Laid low to smiles bought.

In the shadow of Adam
We plant our vines of wine,
Our bodies gathering the sum
Of mental flurries' pine
O'ergrown our fainting head.

I'll streak on down the muddy road,
Taking mud for clothes,
Shying the eyeing laughs
'Til sex shall have no flaws.

RUN, SWEET SMELLS

Gentle rose, gentle rose,
Lend your life to me,
Blossomed in sweet repose,
Gentle rose, gentle rose.

Walking on, walking on,
A city's passioned street,
Spirits walk freshly torn,
Just walking on, walking on.

Gentle rose, gentle rose,
Lend your life to me,
Blossomed in sweet repose,
Gentle rose, gentle rose.

Stopping in, stopping in,
A pub lightly dimmed,
Drinking draught's hope to win,
Just sobbing, sobbing on.

Gentle rose, gentle rose,
Lend your life to me,
Blossomed in sweet repose,
Gentle rose, gentle rose.

Friendly talk, friendly talk,
Playing its unknown tune
While prisoner to life
Just laughs, just laughs too soon.

Gentle rose, gentle rose,
Lend your life to me,
Blossomed in sweet repose,
Gentle rose, gentle rose.

Fitfully, fitfully sleeps my bed
In dreams of hushed lullaby
Gone to lands tears won't wed
'Cause my eyes shed no cry.

Gentle rose, gentle rose,
Lend your life to me,
Blossomed in sweet repose,
Gentle rose, gentle rose.

FOOTPRINTS

When you walk,
Keep a well-meant, well-studied pace
For a man's walk is shown through his face.

When you walk, walk alone;
Greatness shines
When the pace has grown.

This footprint emblazoned and engraved
In the steady and measured beat of time
Is as the tingling juice of lime.
(Never insipid, never enslaved
In the throngs of rushing enclave.)

Ever walked a little traveled path
To suddenly become engrossed
In some footprints in sand?

How your eyes sauntered and stayed
On those footprints impounded in sand.
As each footprint goes from eye, mind, and to hear.

Just as some ancient and fresh-dug art,
Each footprint in this epochal present
Of such ancient seems to impart.
(Impart some unlearned sense of grace
As from print to print our eye is wanton to race.)

Ah, concrete and asphalt jungle,
You encroach upon the social scene,
Making all lives seem a jumble.
(For each walk along the path of life
Our sense of newness skips what's seen.)

Son, when you walk,
Walk in the presence of grace
So your footprints
In some distant, unchartered sand
May mend the threads in life's unraveling lace.

Ever watched the feet on some much-traveled street,
Such a monologue of an unfelt beat,
Clip-clop, clip-clop, clip, clip, clip-clop,
Hurrying on to some unknown, much-chartered sea,
Ever ready to hand out some untutored fee.

When your walk, point in the proper degree;
Footprints emblazoned in the sand
Take life, make life, mold life,
For purpose is always shining in an apogee,
In fruition even in an apostate land.

When you walk, walk alone;
Others will take cue and handle the hone.
It takes faith, fidelity, and courage
To walk on the sands of home.

CHANGE

Swapped me a dollar
For four quarters.

Took off nighties
In exchange for trousers.

Pulled my teeth
For a set of falsies.

Changed my smile
For a fretting frown.

Smoked straights
But now it's filters.

Killed my crabgrass,
Sowed other seeds.

Got me an automatic
Instead of the wringer.

Threw out the woodstove
And got me an electric.

Gave away my black-and-white,
Got me a set with color.

Liked my roomy cuffs,
The slims are lovely.

Held to the one faith,
Found it had changed,
Swapped for another,
Bumped a brick wall.

Had my virility,
Wanted clipped cords.

Wife gave up the ghost,
Wanted my virility,
Doctor said no chance;
Wished my flesh to bawl.

Found that change
In things not to be
Has taste of bitter gall.

Gave back all my change,
Save the remaining three.
My faith in God
Had fled the tee.

Cocreator,
I could never more be.

Change has its folly;
Who's the mind
To fondle this holly?

INDY GOODLIGHT

Page of writ,
Gone, gone to pennied shame
Down rapidy underfilled stream
To river's full though listless note
Carried on to half-sea bay.

Tales, tales hid under salty silt,
Guarded o'er by phosphor eyes
Not in want of telling teach
Yet ever zealous to tale's bide
As taught in sting of anemone.

Ah, these arts of men,
Plied in pennies' store,
Teach their tales in other realms
To future morn prodding, why?

Why build house so high
In catch of underlings breath?
Why great state so sworn to politics
With law staled in sting?
Why great court in matters supreme
Smash the spirit of Indy Goodlight,
Cried in palm of Indy Goodsight?

Gone, gone to invisible bosom
Laid beneath shores of salty silt
To once more in future to blossom
By those same walls not tumbled down
In those thoughts once and fore'er built;
Though in changing lusts,
The page fears ring of other bell
Rung in belfry by Indy Goodlight,
Cried in streets by Indy Goodsight.
Quaint old memory banks.

Dusty roads, dusty roads,
In my childhood youth gone by,
Taking me back to stable home,
Home of eight, each all loved.

Dusty roads, dusty roads,
In my memory, rain-washed ruts
Swelling joy of tars for yesteryear
As old dusty roads wear and wear on by.

Dusty roads, dusty roads,
Cuddled by envious heart
Nongrieved by yester's torn leaf,
Finding its place in moments apart
From the smiles in bundled sheaf.

Dusty roads, dusty roads,
Of childhood mudding place,
All as one, everyplace;
Though fears gone by smear the page,
The page of summer dusty roads.

Dusty roads, dusty roads,
Camera's photo yellowed o'er
By loving fingers touched to gloss,
The gloss of loving sewn cloth
Worn in corners by homey grace;
The grace weathered well through the years
Beaten deep in the ruts of dusty roads,
Those quaint old memory banks.

IGNOBLE NOBLEMAN

How odd, how odd,
You little onion head,
Not the least pretty
'Mongst the onion kin,
Lying in wait for better days,
Feasting 'pon nature food
Before dancing fonder dance.

Kindly hands unclothe the sheath
As lowly sod flakes the germ
That resurrects mighty ego.

White and yellow streak your rod
Till air, wind, and sun
Chord your birthing song.

With mind mightier than man,
Knowing when to spread
Forth a building of worth,
Growing quietly, noisily,
Yet disturbing none.

Your budding trunk
In anxiety's throes
Awaits the sunning table
Touched in angelic gossamer
For tulips tall fable.

Bees in buzzing mirth
Dance 'round quickened bud;
They too have anxiety's touch,
They're nature's fabled farmer
Loved in nature house.

The plant-man of onion heads
Sighing, oh, ah, ah, oh,
As tulips rehearse
Fore opening night.

This plant-man in audio of play
Lets out pent-up ego
In full-blossomed display.

Seeing, touching, and smelling
Beautied bosom breached bare,
Wouldst anyone but fair,
Critique this cathedral of God.

THE WORK SORE BUM

I plant my 'matoes, nuts, and corn
When nature's good to me.

Crows, birds, insects, and flies,
Hail, wind, and gales,
Take my portion profiting me,
Leaving labor work half-paid.

Grass and weeds, mice and moles
Think they're helping hand, free,
Spading my ground and plowing my field
Just where my crop grows prettily.

Disease and wilt, droughts and dry spells
Take a portion from hungry mouth.

Fertilizer and soda, manure and straw
Pamper leaching soil.

Plow and horse, spade, combine and hoe
Bleed my savings unto credit
'Cause human hands of broken bow
Sell not arrows of wit.

I take my portion from greedy bower
And thank all my helping hands free
Though they with eye in greeting sour,
Steal from a bum like me.

SESTINA TO PRESIDENT REAGAN

As sperm and egg clash, sounding even unto God's throne,
There be a fate of leadership determined
For future stir of this celestial spinning footstool
By which the feet of God heavily holds the governed
A little while at rest, a little while in test,
Whether obedience be for common good or ego's wrest.

Throughout life, good and evil look for a moment to wrest
The reigns, the thongs, the scepter, and crown on someone's throne
Held either by consent or intrigue, to brains' or brawn's test,
In rule by word or army the law as determined;
But intrigue or consent has the goodwill of those governed
Far from the power and person holding fast the footstool.

Each day there's battle to move the chair away from the footstool
With a word passed at table by the cowardly in wrest
From the person that truth, faith, and honor placed by the governed,
Who protect against wavering in the winds of the throne
The one in rule, so fairly and mightily determined,
That principle, though they only be, shall wring the day's test.

The foxes may have their woods and the birds their sky in test
Separate in conflicts dyed in the fabric on footstool,
For each to have a say and each a will as determined,
Which the tool, the hour, and which the method in play of wrest
How grand, how lovely, one would begat or dress the throne
In the fates of leadership so controlled by the governed.

Each time there comes the fate of vote psyched by the governed
In put to rest the awesome trial of leadership's test,
There are those battles, though to good or evil, at the throne
That subjects would so fondly stay or remove from footstool
The leader would perfume or so unkindly try to wrest
That faith and hope the votes so loyally determined.

DE TI HE WA

Listen, my child, I'll tell your mind of nationhood.
You tell your child, and he tell his forevermore
Of friends to love and enemies of hate withstood
The precious grinding stone ahoning freedom's score.
Cutting through all jangled paths to treachery's door
Locked against entreaties. Freedom offers its wood.
There're wails in some darksome demon's evil hell lore,
Escaping not till freedom pities sorrow's whore
In wedlock to traitor renewed by sons of four.

(My child listened to his grandfather's truthful tale.)

History was floating on its bark in tepid seas
When a people was their freedoms in anchored waves
Too much troubled by a monster in its seethes,
Swirling fins, digging hole 'round about anchor staves,
Two centuries long stood in pounding angry waves
In currents, long on bleating froth, seething the lees,
Fermenting an anger against the tow of freedom slaves;
Then pounding that which freedom sees
In sight of traitor wishing fail of liberties.

(My child blinks an eye as he stares the stormy scene.)

This monster so lochnessed, so ghostly, ghastly aride,
Channels its spy to unlock the secrets held
Upon escarpment on the gentle forthright tide
This nation ever holds in arms, though tides have felled.
More mighty than her two centuries jelled,
Jelled with pains and hurts, but still in freedom cried,
"Up, up from despairing depths, the bell hasn't knelled
For keepers from the frothy depths to thrash its tide
Against a nation rose from birth a-walk worldwide."

(My child was taken up into this stormy scene.)

Like all weepers agathered by graveside mound,
Monsters spray a dream, look and hook their thoughts waved
Upon naughts and boughs a traitor jingles acrowned,
Thinking freedom shall one day float on seas depraved,
To die awhile then rise to some ignoble ways craved;
Stalwart journeymen, in askance sunset afrowned,
"Why silver line our clouds if clouds to rains have bathed
In freedom gone aseek without a freedom bound,
Reveled to grazing pawns, renewed on traitor's ground?"

(My child, deep in thought, wondered why the clouds had come.)

It's then a peoples alooked their olden corals
To see their anchor a bit removed from its place
Of lushful meadows grazed by trusty shants and shalls,
Where the weight line of ship is marked and kissed with grace
By its sail upon the swelling tides of freedom's embrace,
Dancing spirits, childed in birth by guys and gals,
Ensuring freedom shall upon the human race
Live awhile until spirits thrown from evil pals
Shall cause a cause to creak and break its freedom calls.

(My child, bleary eyes, sought the mean of swelling tides.)

Then in the dust ancestors had grit to grind,
A call had come from graves with blow of trumpet blares
To shake the fetor fetters would perfume and wind
About, around, every riser to freedom's stairs,
As if the loathsome tune all traitors load with cares
Should lead wondrous song of freedom into its blind,
Carefully scraped, with disrupting vines' scareful tares,
To prick, to sore, to fester all of freedom kind
When apathy opened doors freedom left behind.

(My child, grow not weary; freedom's histories tell.)

Oh, come, you blind, you depraved, see beauty displayed
Away from your tangled, misty dreamed amours.
See the plight you wish on others cruelly dismayed,
Where you in midst of offspring, who came to these shores,
Deny the labors, the sweat of those in their snores,
Who ran to death rather than freedom disobeyed.
'Tis now you in armored death bury their folklores
In honor, not treaties, binding their honors prayed,
So you could have chance to color their freedoms grayed.

(My child told me he'd be counted among the brave.)

Look back, look back, and stumble not in those pools of blood
That your ancestors shed into nobility,
Whose armored trust at reading often through the mud
Of strangest traitor paths lacking salinity,
Embroiled, inscribed, enthroned upon idolatry,
Rushing in traitor mind, snipping at freedom's bud.
Traitors belie all beauty ever wished in free
Souls like diamonds sparkling in most precious stud,
Freeing blood, blood, blood for freedom and its cud.

(My child whispered to me, "I understand what's true.")

Look back again, this nation's cities flamed and torn.
Consider well the wage all traitors rip from lathe,
The starting line begun to praise the efforts born
In those more noble, more enthroned in freedom's crave,
To lay their lives with its most precious booty, brave
Into the streams, whose watered paths look not forlorn,
But tryst the effort as held rein came to bathe.
While the mist of freedom walked on through waving corn,
Above the graves all traitors are flowered with freedoms.

("My child," I told him, "you're in freedom loved and born.")

My child would look back again on down freedom's road
To West if opportunity beckoned him
From shore long stood mankind's trample and goad;
Away he wagoned across dust and plains so grim
While juggernauts so weighed and hampered his joy's brim
Of finding the tiled albatross' soulful load,
That arrows and sun and dust beneath moonlight dim
Had mostly conquered his freedom-thirsty abode
Until his God reached out and found his freedom sowed.

(My child asked me in wonder, "What is freedom sowed?")

I tell you once more, my child, to look back again.
Traitors revel in throes of flesh's awful sod,
Galloping, strangling death, if danger has gain
Of fleeting feathered hat pulled hard 'gainst freedom's nod;
Yet traitors know their flames pit freedom 'gainst them hard,
Turning their galloping steed into optioned pain,
Kicking, yearning, burning to quench freedom's rod,
Rethreaded in hearts that only traitors dare to feign
When tasting death or rubbing freedom 'gainst its grain.

(My child looked up into my eyes and smiled at me.)

To your grand ones do tell them this: my child of earth,
Great explorers came in quest flight of eagle wings,
Fluttering, excitedly fluttering, for berth,
Where none but bravery's council in freedom sings,
Adieu to traitors and the fires treachery brings,
To light a flame here, a commotion there in mirth,
Spreading revolution with their ting-ting-a-lings,
As if the heart knows not how truer freedom rings.

(My child said, "Freedom! Freedom, freedom evermore!")

My child, I must remind you of trials you'll face,
Of burdens sure to come as you face fears and scares
Along the road you and nation travel or pace.
There're rocks and stones and boulders too to fret your cares.
There traitors hide behind the trees to take your wares,
To make your nation's bravest freedoms stand in waste.
Be stalwart, be strong against their dark, hidden lairs.
There's more to a pudding than flavor put by mace,
More to nationhood than freedom's protected place.

(My child asked, "Why do we have to die for freedom?")

Before I tuck you in covers of freedom's arm,
There's more to say, but you, my child, cannot bear it's tale.
I ask you, over the graves to sing freedom's calms,
It's worthy to honor those lived in freedom's dell,
To gather its flowers bloomed by abyss of hell,
Yet never looking in that darkened river's qualms
That traitors are so true to then die in her yells,
Smiling the day when freedom, perchance, alarms
Those heroes' graves in succor the living with freedom's balms.

(De Ti He WA. He waited. The old man tucked him
Into bed, all covered with lace of freedom's trim.
He dreamed, sweetly dreamed, that freedom was still swim.
The old man who tucked the bed was freedom—he, him.)

GRIEVING SUNS

Work is but a spell that binds
The cruelest thought to pleasant times.
Blue morn sprinkled on the sky,
Sorrow licks at bed that grieves,
And chilling heart has frozen up,
Wishing day had barked its pup.

Work in but a spell that binds
Wished to spend the golden dime,
Time to sing songs in the sun,
Lack of work spent in the shade
And drinks the spirit far beyond
Thought of work ne'er too fond.

Work all you can—youth of life,
Strong ones have never counted time
For one worshipped hour in sun.
Old ones long for work that's lost,
And for the golden years of youth,
Work is but a blinding truth.

FROM START TO STAR

Each year at Christmastide,
Santa and I across the deserts ride;
We sprinkle stardust here
   and soul lust there
Into hearts unborn and bare.

We smell the flower of wisdom's brush.
We ponder the coat of the brown, brown thrush.
We listen to the hooves of people hide
To bring the magic of Christmastide
Before the land has withered and died.

Our souls have longed for boredom's rest,
We feast our hearts in the crib's good nest
And bell our minds to chime the kingdom come,
Hopeful the beds shall change upon the dumb
As Jesus, Mary, and I offer a crumb
From the works of Joseph's faith in heaven come.

Ere the night draws to a comatose close,
And the curtains to windows are froze;
Santa and I ride for that star
Held in the hands of Hesch and Carr,
Val, Kauffman, Schmied, and Pitt,
For in their hands is a written note
Sent by one with a song in his throat.

Santa's not too loving in the house of the poor,
That's why I go and knock on their door.
There is someone who will give them much more
Than a toy to break and a rag on the floor.
Jesus will bring a soul full of store
To wipe their tears forevermore
With a smile and of grace outpour.

Come on, Santa, let's take a ride,
I'm all for smelling the flowers' pride;
The wind is cold with a nip outside.
Jesus has a warmth that has never died.
With his swaddling cloth of joy this Christmastide,
Let's go to the gilded, the gifted and fielded,
Their joy too we shall have milled it.

FORWARD

I see my sunsets as yesterday's
Thousand-paged book,
Thousand-paged book become one word.

Much read, much trimmed, much played,
Much traveled and trailed pathway
Through all hearts pulsating love.

Love is my sunset riding on,
Galloping through my yesterday's
Rustic pathway with many trails.
Love, if love be a word,
Brings my yesterdays to trial
In these, my gloried sunsets,
Shining on my ivy by the road.

DUST STORMS

Roadsides in countrysides
Spray the mind with wanton mists,
Sweeten the sounds and colors
Of wild nature lisps,
Bringing to journeyman
Walking in its midst.

Roadsides in countrysides
Hide the mystery at bend;
There's not what the mind had thought,
Greeting a journeyman
At the roadside's end.

REDUNDANCY

Man is not alone;
With a candle and a match,
His heart the fonder beats
Within his clovered catch.

Durations as moments
Float o'er his sweet, hayed patch,
Due moments as time
Moss the thatch
'Til the candle,
Smaller, shies the match.

GLEAN-SPIN

I'm a gleaner, a gleaner,
In the fields, the fields,
The fields of the Lord.
He has sowed the seed
Of salvation
In the fertile fields of God.

Is my seed asprouting,
Asprouting in the walk,
The walk he has begun
Along the road,
The road of heaven talk.

(refrain)

Roots, tares, and climate
Paint the picture,
The picture of brighter hue,
When we're a cultivating,
Cultivating the fields of the Lord.

(refrain)

At the harvest,
At the harvest time,
He will crack my hull,
My hull of seed,
And mill it to flour,
Flour of whitest bleed.

(refrain)

THE TENDENCY

Plausible meeting,
This savage embryonic cry,
Torn between the leaf of life
And the leaf of will to die.

Shout the way-song,
Walk the banner high,
We tread not the way long
Nor see the leaf in sky.

From no leaf
To new leaf
To old leaf
Colored by life,
This the plausible meeting
Of leaf, leaf living to die.

Shout the way-song
To the leaf of life,
Walk its banner high;
Tread not the way long
To the leaf of will to die,
Look up, look up, look up,
And see a leaf in sky.

BANEFUL WHIM

Flea-bitten dog crossed my path
On way to garden to push my wrath
On those wormy potatoes
And rotten cabbageheads.

No stranger to me but a stranger to him,
He pursed a leg and left a film
Right there on Big Boy so pretty and prim.

That flea-bitten dog tucked a leg
When I called him
Wormy potatoes and rotten cabbagehead.

I hoed the weed and smelled the flowers
Of possum Jim and Mary in Tijuana;
That damn dog chased a mole in its towers,
Oh, three of us drunk on flowers.

The flea-bitten dog
Howled a whim
At a mockingbird
Mocking out on a limb.

The detowered mole
Plowed my garden through,
Wilting my hundredfold
To only game he knew.

I laughed at the dog
Biting flea-bitten flesh,
I sang to the fog
Of the mockingbird's mesh;
My hoe, as a flog,
Pounded the mole in duress
While possum Jim and Mary in Tijuana
Laughed at me
In wanton of a cress.

VULGARITY

what are vulgar words
but interpreter thereof.
what are vulgar actions
but eye staying too long.
what are vulgar deeds
but gossip well fed.
what are vulgar pictures
but mind in absent state.
what is vulgar love
but each to expression's way.
what is vulgar religion
but freedom's nongain say.
What are we
but compunction's weight.

WEE TIME TO SELF

Take my hand, dear one,
Let's walk love's fair lane.
Let's wash our ivory clean.
Let's hear the dove's clear call.
Let's learn of self overruled.
Let's throw our hearts to the wind.
Let's clean our whipping post.
Let's linger in courtship long.
Let's not rush wedding song's sour note.
Let's part our ways of one desire.
Let's live our lives in sweet, sure rest.

Take me heart, dear one,
If love's fair lane passes by.
If desires are warm and clean.
If the heart goes pitter patter.
If each heart bends to love's caress.
If faults melt the fat of life.
If desires cause not duress.
If flesh steals not conscience's hold.
If plans be forevermore.
If print of life soothes the qualms.
If forever be forevermore.

SUNSET AND EVENSONG

In the cool of the evening,
      the Spirit walks about,
'Twas told in the beginning

God was at walk
      in the cool of the evening,
In the cool of the evening
      our spirit tasks the day.

In the cool of the evening,
      at time of sunset's evensong,
Our work is at cease,
      the soul grapples its peace,
The day has been wearisome and long.

The evening comes as drink
      to a thirsty soul,
The wind tires in chase
      the elements,
The birds grow happy in rest
      from search of food,
The grasses rejoice
      in tears of dew;
All nature knows
      evening's a time of brood
To shout amen to God
      in the evensong of sunset new.

Shout my soul to God in song,
Praise his will for the day's good done,
Thresh the dine of friendship known
In this sunset and evensong.

If a sunset never came
To cool man's spirit
           in the heat of blame,
Would there be time for God
In the sweat of tilling the sod?
Would there be sunset and evensong
To cool the breeze and thoughts of toil
Before the hands touched
                    the daily soil?

THE NASHVILLE GLOW

I'm going to Nashville
And listen guitars thrill
Me on a mountain hill.
Those songs will ever fill
Me for my lovely Lil
There on a mountain hill.

I met her in Dundas
That moment upon us
Showered us with stardust.
Those winds of mountain gust
Whispered to me, I must
Go to Nashville or bust.

I asked her would she go.
She whispered, "I don't know."
But sure as winds that blow,
I must see Nashville glow,
Guitars that strum so low,
"I love you, love you so."

With no reservations,
With no reservations,
I sing recitations
Of love's celebration.
There were no frustrations—
Just Nashville's vibrations.

THE STAINED PAIR OF SHOES

Some fancy tanner stained my shoe of life
Much before echoes reverberate these walls
Wherein secrets are told in some spirit's falls,
Walking in someone's shoe of life.

Stains from a stained shoe of life
May tiptoe on carpeted floors,
Hearing drums loudly cadenced in dance
Vanishing carpet from cold tiled floors,
Like an osprey tearing freedom's blood,
Leaving bleached white bones on the floor of life.

Stop here awhile in that stained shoe of life;
Compose your lyrical song in all motioned range.
See the lily racing to bloom
Before the rapper dresses to other mind change.
Hear the strained battle, fierce, in the shoe of life.

Loosen those straps on your stained shoes of life,
Fear not to cry whether to sadness or joy;
The mold must have its moisture to sap every dreg.
Play your actor or actress endeared to script's role,
Now's the time to shed the stained shoe of life.

Get mad and change that stained shoe of life
But not before it's walked the last heavy mile.
There are tears to be shed and laughs to be enjoyed.
There are words to be reworked and style to be changed.
There are habits to be shaken to the last bare thread
Before walking out of that stained shoe of life.

Walk one last time in that stained shoe of life
Through muddles of mud, floods, and desert sands.
Tire yourself well—get it out of craw,
Scratch, bite and fight, cry and laugh a little joy,
This the last time memories shall feign.
Strong are the rusted links in life's chain
When walking out of a stained pair of shoes to life.

      (Dedicated to all those who would pour the stains
      Out of their life and walk in a beautiful pair
      Of shoes into their quest to blossom their
      Joy and thrill of life.)

THE SALUTING HEART

Somewhere there're rainbows' gold pots
    Sitting in sunsets' gold streams
Far, far away like small dots
As the mind supplies the lots
    Only in the eyes as dreams.

One may travel farther, wide,
    In search of the golden pathway
As thoughts come only to hide
The soul's longing to confide
    The pain of each echoed bye.

Foxes may climb mountains high
    In search golden scenes beyond––
Summit tells the dream is dry,
And clouds go floating on by,
    Scanning home's sweet magic wand.

There be gold in turtle's stride
    Though last to glean o'erworked fields;
Still there be a lurking pride
Where other's dreams have past, died,
    Seeing gold that ne'er fulfills.

Travelers see all views past
    And ne'er can tell where rest is
'Til there comes a vision fast
And draws the heart to its cast
    That fields of home's always best.

THE POOLS OF SWIMMING SELVES

Yon Ethraim Fearshaker

Every person born on earth
a student to another's worth;
matters not the lesson's tilt
when calmness soothes the cloudy silt,
but somehow a word can smother
if tongued as love of a mother
loving lesson instead of child.

Every will to a person born
can be chopped and twisted and torn,
and matters not the will as lent
when ball and chain cannot be bent
and never prison dug is dark and deep,
never the will back to owner seep.

Every birth is a death on earth
to promise of a soul in mirth;
matters not the turn and toggle,
swaddling cloths to others snuggle
'til the burner has parched its mark
and given life to death in silent spark.

Every death is a life on earth,
giving substance to a berth
blazoned on a daily anvilled chorus,
beaten to visions vibrantly porous
until there be time no more
in separate that seed from core.

ORATIONS DIMMED

O God, you the spreader of days,
Vigor, truth, and happiness,
All are e'er your ways.
We, the gleaners of those days,
Have many thoughts to tell,
Have broken collar stays to mend
And perchance have blossoms in our lapels.

The truth, you are of our long years,
Brighten our lives with tales of joy
And happiness fulfilled,
Falling 'pon your gift, our ears,
We wish to hold dear and so finely milled.

How the mystery of friendship's shining eve,
If not by your beholden sleeve gathering
All our old yet new tales of regret, as we
Recall your memories tucked und' our warmed
O'er sweet apathies, regenerated anew in us,
As words break open our divining rod,
And we see those words e'er so clear
Sewn in our lives' much-sewn seam.

THE CLOCK OF CAPISTRANO

Yon E. Fearshaker

Let me out, you time;
let me hear your cockle-combed
shout beyond your mesh-wired frame.
If there be spurs to shunt my passing ego,
let your ball and chain speak the hour come;
there be more to arrow-pointed hands
than repealing, repeating, reverberating
tick-tock, tock-tick out from that
box of walnut wood.
       Speak the mind of you, created innards,
as more than an inventor's dream
bent upon hypnotism's school;
there be more to your time and tune
than eons of sculptured volumes of writ.
There's silted through the sun, sand, and surf
a cog spring of one eternal wind
when the shy cuckoo awakes the half-time note
there be lantern with fossil life enough
to flicker the swallowed hour upon Capistrano;
but still the clock must tock the tick as when
the cuckoo graced not its perch,
and Capistrano lifts its image in mirage
to counter the clockwork's eternal wind
true to the forgers of brass, gold, and iron
of creation's inlayed walnut wood.

WHY IS IT

Why is it or should it be
that money's a changing tree?
Why is it and should it be
deals are found at golf's last tee?
There it is or is it there,
that thing market says is flair?
There it is or was it there,
monies' worth while sitting chair?
When you purchase all commodes,
new fashions close all your roads,
and undies shy your commodes
like see-throughs weren't à la modes.
Where deals are or should deals be
competing e'er so fiercely,
and your deals are left to be
on the block of bankruptcy?
Say you will or should you say,
I'll bet my alfalfa hay
if my horses do not say,
I'm not running good today.
But
if tomorrow's like today,
I'll sell my commodes and say,
"Change the à la modes today
and inventory the hay!"

DOOMS AWAY

Of all the things in the sky,
there's nothing like a cloud floating by,
and if there's lazy time to lavish a bit,
wash your mind in their dancing vapored flit.
Find the cause of your parched of thirst
before you drown in the cloudy burst,
then you'll see wispy clouds fading away,
and there's nothing but sunshine
the rest of day;
when you see a cloud floating by,
let not its gray gather into black.
You're in command each skyway track.

EASTER IS FOR RESURRECTION

E^b B^b E^b B^b

(refrain)

Easter is for resurrection,
         G^m a^7 B^b
Our love and our joy and our dreams,
E^b F^7 B^b
Those friendships and those affections
F^7 E^b F^7 B^b
Lifting our lives into their streams.

(verses)

Children have their Easter egg hunts;
Others see a bloom in their lives.
Easter bunnies come with their stunts,
And all love, joy, and peace arrive.

(refrain)

Nature buds a joy in its leaves.
Our souls are lifted out beyond
And gather love into our sleeves
To make a special Easter bond.

(refrain)

Then angels sing, "He is risen
To fill all your love, joys, and dreams,
And friendship once more will christen
The love flowing in all your streams.

(refrain)

181

TALKING TO MY SWEET

G   D⁷ C

(refrain)

Chirping in my heart
G   D⁷ C
Where melodies start
D⁷ G⁷
Is an Easter dart
D⁷   G
Sent to my sweetheart.

(verses)

Walking down the street,
Kissing as we meet,
Talking to my sweet,
Dancing at my feet.

(refrain)

We know no other,
We are as lover
Without no druthers
While love does hover.

(refrain)

> My love for my date,
> Easter's celebrate.
> Need we ever wait
> To sing of our fate.

(refrain twice)

December 10, 1986

EVERYBODY'S BLUES

(refrain)

I have heard it all before;
You came knocking on my door.
I'm gonna even the score,
you, you two by two by four.

(verses)

You caught me in the bedroom
Using my heavy perfume.
You couldn't even presume
The light went out in the room.

You took me to marry
And my faults to carry.
You made me so scary
When you sunk my ferry.

I just couldn't do no right.
You quarreled with me each night
And called it lover's fight.
I say it just ain't right.

I raised the kids for you.
I wasn't honeydew.
You said it was too few.
Listen here, I'm gonna sue.

Get your things outta here,
Your whiskey and your beer.
Don't wait to call me dear,
I've had it up to here.

SINGING THOSE NASHVILLE SONGS

(Refrain)

    G   D^7 G^7 D^7 G D^7 G
There's clapping and yelling from one and all
    G^7 D^7 G
Singing their songs in Grand Ole Opry hall,
   D^7 G^7 D^7 G D^7 G
Hearing those songs the greats have made so tall,
   D^7 G   G^7 D^7 G
da-de, da-de de-dum, de-tum, de-dall.

(verses)

   G D^7 G D^7 G^7 G
Acuff is singing for the Great White Dove.
   D^7 G   D^7 G D^7
Minnie Pearl is joking all for love.
   G   D^7 G
Four guys are singing like angels from above,
D^7 G   G^7 D^7
And that's Nashville on the wings of a dove.

(refrain)

Boxcar Willie's out stopping all the trains
Before Merlin Husky sings in the rain
To Mother Maybelle still humming refrain
To Hank Williams living in songs so plain.

(repeat refrain)

Many will come to replace the many who've gone
To sing on shores of heaven breaking dawn.
Their songs will remain after stars have drawn
Their last hurrahs, and guitars are for pawn.

(repeat refrain)

So let us sing those songs of worth untold
Of the weak, the scarred, the brave, and the bold,
And sing our songs for those out in the cold.
The Grand Ole Opry shall never grow old.

TAKE YOUR DRUGS AWAY

(refrain)

Won't you take your drugs away,
Go and throw them all out the door?
I don't want your possum play
Asleep in my bed anymore.

(verses)

I know you're courting Mary,
Mary Juanta. It's so scary.
You're always in a hurry
To perfume the r——m with curry.

You were my favorite weed.
Now there are no roses or bead;
There's only your thirsting need,
And to my love you do not heed.

You're not drunk of alcohol,
But that too you've got to let fall.
I'm tired of sitting to bawl
Because of your drugs, drugs and all.

Can't tell you what I will say,
But I'm going far away
If you do not cease to play
With those drugs that get in our way.

LIVING TOGETHER

(refrain)

If today you love me as ever,
The vows we made will never sever
Love and trust of living together.
There'll be a rose on every thorn,
And living together will be born.

(verses)

Our walk through the woods shall not be dark.
Those trees we carve will be love's own mark.
The path we walk will be love's own park,
And fire will flame with our love's own spark.

Our trust of each other will live on.
Those moments of darkness shall not mourn.
Our love of each other has no scorn,
And living together will be born.

It's not so bad to live together,
Trying to guess each other's weather.
The wind that blows today and clouds up
Tomorrow will be well on the way
To help us live better together.

VOLUNTATIS

I saw my Christmas star
Beaming rays over my faith;
If each ray could penetrate
The darkness within the soul,
There'd be a Christmas star
Guiding us in heaven's way.

(refrain)

What would Christmas be
Without th'announcing star,
Without th'angel tide
Of gloria, gloria,
Gloria in excelsis Deo.

(refrain)

I heard the church in reply:
Et in terra pax hominibus
voluntatis, voluntatis—
There'll be voluntatis in terra
When we follow the Gloria Star.

(refrain)

I looked up and saw
The star had gone,
The crib had turned to dust;
His mother told me
And angels accented in reply:
Someday his love will return,
And we'll have another Christmas star
Of gloria, gloria, gloria,
Alleluia, gloria in terra.

(refrain)

WHERE THE ROAD DIVIDES

Where the road divides
And the heart faints a spell,
The body pulls a weight
Pushed by dusty dust of love.

Where the road divides
To equation's weight,
The mind grips a line
In tow the mingled fate.

Where the road divides
To the rise and set of sun,
No one sits in deride
Time's fruit thus won.

Where the road divides
To heaven's bliss,
There's the parting ways
To hell's offered kiss.

Where the road divides
To dividing road,
The road divides
To going ways.

The going ways
May divide the road,
But where the road divides,
We leave a burdened load.

THE BLUSHING PALLOR

Like the clay so red
Blushing for the mountaintop
Is a blush come to the face
In the company of friendship's bloom
When mountaintop denies a place.

The clay, never at mountaintop,
In tire of blush
Mates with sand-washed loam
In hunger friendship's meal.

Lighter, lighter, grayer still,
The once red clay blushes again
The meal sought, said without grace,
Brings not the thrill of blush,
Brings not a thrill to face.

The once red clay bows to prophecy:
A daily bide is not the friend;
Artichokes lose their sheen
In destiny's overcooked pot.

FREE ME, O BLESSED SAVIOR

Free me, free me, O Blessed Savior,
Free me from the bonds of sin's deadly tree;
I struggle, I struggle, O how I struggle
To keep thy grace within.

The road is wide leading to sin's deadly tree,
Many, there are many falling prey
To the ruts within.

The door, the door to thy grace
Is ever, ever open to me
Behind the confessional door;
Blessed Savior, I thank thee,
I thank thee for the keys
Which open heaven's door to me.

Blessed words, those blessed words,
Making my soul skip with glee,
When I hear, I absolve thee.

MY PINCH OF SALT

Ah, the mores of man
Diversely laden
Caressly endured
Burden world's full gunnysack
Placed on merchant's shelf
Never bought for sell,
Just thought bag of sentiments
Dried hard by yearning crust
Envied by all prying eyes
As each possessed his fill
In crying hands and outstretched arms
Craven to elements sacked therein
Ever blossomed to mind,
Yet bud in action fails the food
Ground in cultures' hasting mood
Plod e'er so deep in lipped, fouled wound
Whose sore festers deeply round
The running one's smothering pant
Gone grossly imbecile
To mind's unneighbored role
Caustically etched in soul's breath
Flown to wayward signs
Encased in mores' gunnysack,
Unraveling thread by thread
Lain too long in moldy air
Of culture's unsensed mores

Escaping mean of gunnysack
Bought by merchant in horrify,
Thinking he could stop
The cultured mooring path of man
Filtered not in civility's crop
That only each eats the fill
Not as only one in cribbing pan
But as one for all mankind,
Loving in love's true essence
These cultured mores of man
As issued from the gunnysack.

STAIR, LADDER, RUNGS

Up the skywalk
Through the ages,
We shall sing
Our song of love
Up the skywalk
Through the ages,
Clothing, feeding, singing,
Singing joyously
Our medley of love.

Up the skywalk
Through the ages,
Monishing, preaching,
Teaching the amen sound.

Up the skywalk
Through the ages,
Visiting, touching,
Healing hearts broken down.

Up the skywalk
Through the ages,
Alleluia, alleluia,
Christ the victory,
Christ has our crown.

Up the skywalk
Through the ages,
Working, trembling
Beads of sweat
Flood our brow.
Bodies fretting,
Souls regretting,
Day has drawn
Its test of love.

Up the skywalk
Through the ages,
Thunders pealing,
Lightning's crackling,
Sun's a-hiding,
Stars a-falling;
We reap rewarding
We have seen our love.

STUMPED

Why 'tis with grown-ups
They live not by word;
I've been told times o'er
Not to smoke
And lust for gold.

Same mouth that mouthed to me
Spurts its smoke
And fills the house
In antiques and precious motes.

Told to me by parentry:
Do not drink nor mind the sex;
These are ways to eternity.

I've seen down their corridors
Dimly lit in wining bars.
I've seen their public abodes
Soiled without marriage vows.

Wisdomed mouths
Mouth to me
As visitors drop by for see,
"Out to play as children good,
Seen not heard."

Listening through walls:
I wish parents would
'Main as children
Seen not heard.

PASSING THE BUCK

Glowering embers
Forsaken of flame
Wink at hearth
In questioned blame.
Hearth waves in warmth
To embers dressed
In graying shame.
Chimney grows in fame,
Harboring all emplaned
To good-drafted main.

BEST NOT

I had a turtle—slow,
All colored
Orange and black;
Also, had tiny
Sparrow songed
And charcoaled
With white on tips.
Fed him not
A mansion's feast;
He warred
The winged adults
About to make
Mushy garden nest.

My turtle preened
On children, wee,
E'ere holing
Pretty garden dress.

My turtle
Looked at sparrow
Then quickly
Back to me.
I couldn't tell
My turtle
Sparrow more than he.
I couldn't tell
My sparrow
Turtle meant more
To me.

BEST FRIEND

Dogs howl in moonlight
To siren's shrilly tone.

Barking at winds' shadow
Stubbing tail 'tween hind legs.

Biting strangers' shinbones,
Chasing cars delighted heart.

Waning rugs colored bright,
Minding only whip's sting.

Greedily eating scraps
Thrown to other dog yon.

Smelling all dogs' wet trails,
Not minding where they end.

Caring not when time comes
To defend stabled home.

Dogs habits so like men—
When men stop reasoning,
Free will stumbles within.

TICKLED

Tingle my mind,
Spread my lips,
Bare my teeth.

Flourish my nerves,
Quiver my lips,
Shine my teeth.

Vibrate my chords,
Still my lips,
Cover my teeth'
'Tis only a laugh.

IN MY STADIUM

Freedom!
      Freedom,
Do I hear
'Pon winds in vibration
From guitars, saxes,
Fiddles, and groups dear?

Freedom!
      Freedom,
Do I hear
As muscled chirps
Fall on all attends' ear?
Wonder!
      Wonder
If words connote much
In freedom's call here.

Freedom!
      Freedom,
Do I hear
In muscled forest
Of unsociety's peer,
Leaning, leaning
Much too far,
Far from present
Chorused ones,
Bleating, bleating
To ones found arrear?

Freedom!
        Freedom
Does not call
Humans 'pon animal bar:
No words glean
In action played mean
'Pon lonely ones'
Greedy, sissied star.

Freedom!
        Freedom!
Ah, freedom's call;
Musters stadium's
Cease to animal gall.
None for freedom
In freedom's ball:
Call the police,
We'll just sit
In motionless stall.

Freedom!
        Freedom!
Gone to apathy's door,
Gone to weed's path
Flown society's shore,
Gone to sigh in wrath.
Freedom, freedom gone
Fore song told all:
Why gather our bits
In stores of pawn?
Freedom, freedom,
'Tis freedom gone.

DAWN'S LIGHT CHASING TWILIGHT'S DARK

I go
From dawn's light
To twilight's dark,
Chasing dreams
To netherworld.

I come when
Dawn's light stirs
My heart lightly
As heaven's furnace
Quickens ego's staff
Down fruitless paths,
Flesh thought,
Bloomed and fruited.

I sit as
Noontime quakes
In short shadows,
Crushing my pacing steps.

I lay
In spirited shadows
Once at dawn's light,
Trembling in noon's witch,
Sending quaked shadows
Lengthening to dawn's light.

I wake as
Each shadow sends
Its signaled direct
In twain screams
'Pon racer's minted beams.

Must dawns draw
From twilight's dark
Its teach climatic?

Must twilights draw
From each dawn's light
Its bit of wisdom stole?

Must dawns and twilights
Meet at noon
In signal of combat's heat?

Must twilights and dawns
Fade into each
At noon's stopping time?

Must from dawn to twilight
We in labored plans
Sigh direct to frontal plane?

Must from twilight to dawn
We in fretting sleep
Ponder life in sigh?

BIG G

Good morning, love,
How'd your bed fare
With help from above?

Did you sleep your share
Or laid counting dove
As they played in hair?

Good morning, hub,
My, oh My!
With you, my gift, from above.

FLOWN TOO SOON

I saw a robin
Alight upon
Weeny sweet gum tree;
Along came another
I thought matey be.

How still, still
In thoughts
These two robins
Swayed by wind.

In saddened mood
I know not of,
Two robins left their
Sweet-gummed rocking chair
For safer perch
On wind's wavy hair.

If I'm like robin
Not cursed
In natured flair,
Guess I'd have
Longer stayed
In sweet gum's
Rocking chair.

THE PUBLICS' GATHERER

Bring me iris
Fallen o'er by wind,
The wind of public opinion.

Bring me iris
Stampeded by crush,
The crush of opinions' tines.

Bring me iris
Discolored by bee
Anxious in noneties' hug.

Bring me iris
Plucked by roots
In gardener's ill time.

Bring me iris;
I'll list its silent speech—
Silent, but telling all.

My gift of iris
Found a homing ear
'Mongst roses of pride.

My iris through action told
'Tis not by word
Public senses mold.

CRIPPLED DEN

Thatch my roof with tumbleweeds,
Patch my wall with adobe brick.
Dig my well to denizens' den,
Burn crude oil 'pon cottoned wicks.
Wet my lips in cacti sweat,
I poor traveler in wagon's zest.

Leak my roof with desserts' grin,
Burst my wall in gale wind.
Dry my well upon demons' fire,
Rot my wicks in drying air.
Parch my lips 'pon mirage's glass;
My old horse better last,
Pulling its old traveler
In search of wagon's zest.

Pour, ye prairie rains, pour,
Howl, ye ill winds, blow;
Fill my well to sure crops' grow,
Burn ye olden wick
Scorched in afterglow.
Sing my lips in newborn songs—
'Tis the West
This poor traveler longs.

TRAITOR

I've a treasure trove
Picked for blossom in home.
My hands caressed its perfume
In love's e'er-changing flame.
I placed my blossom
In love's full-watered jar,
Fresh from life's spring.

Grown so used to blossom in vase,
I one day called it Sweet Johanna.
Much to my surprise,
Blossom fades in blush
Only to quickly surmise
Vows in wed's sweet crush.

TURNING O'ER

Leave the day straw
To nesting birds of prey,
Cut my forested
O'ergrown simple way.

Bind the day straw
Some days from hence;
Gather in my shakes
Tangled in barbed repents.

File the day straw
High of meager days,
Store my wanderings
others changing amaze.

DISGRUNTLED

Work my fingers to the bone,
Sitting in comfy chair
'Hind desk too big for one.

Point my finger to receptionist
And say in tired tone,
"Clients can wait another day,
For now, I'll sit all alone."

Squinch my face to janitor hired.
"Scrub the walls and dust the floor,
Visitors come to much admire
My office too big for one."

Shake my finger in governor's face
'Cause he likes his hand in pot
Fore I get my fair share.

Twist my finger to accountant there;
He thins my padding,
Seeing need for another chair.

Darned I'll sit this chair all day,
Doing jobs of ones I hired.
Give me granny nest
And make me comfy fire.

THE FOYER

Oh man,
Do you remember
Not so long ago
That you set forth
Some fertile
Soil to grow?
'Twas the longest
Path you ever trod
By nature's work
Of growing sod.

Some had paths
With flowerets
Along the way,
But you in haste
Made scent go astray,
Too long in waiting
To abide
The much-known path,
Sometimes even begging
Nature's growling wrath.

The foyer,
If it may
Be called as such,
Stung the nostrils
With an unkindly
Though common touch.

Those clothes
Made with modern clasps,
Proof that man
Has a quickening grasp
That brings, ofttimes,
Resounding joy at last.

Three eyes gape at you
In welcome attire;
This is your moment
Of need so dire
As you sit
Upon one hole
And sort of perspire
As the bugle sounds
Forth the call:
One filled,
Two for hire.

Even the cows
In the meadow,
Chewing the cud,
Look in amazement
At such, at such
An unmannerly crud
For even you make
Their bellowing
Sound as a dud
As you in haste
Make unsightly mud.

The hands reach forth
For the book of ads
As the eye glances
At the pretty fads;
Nature has triumphed
As the bowels make glad.

Oh man,
To the past
You must look back:
'Tis a blessing
No longer
Must you make tracks
To that small foyer
Of all seasons' clime,
Sort of hid
In the hedges
Way yon in the back.

IVY BY THE ROAD

I see my sunsets as yesterday's
Life-filled moments mingled into one
Great cistern giving all its sweet taste.
Enmity smothered by life's total friends
Grins 'round yon corner as life amends
Treachery in styled plumes
Treading to cultured amens.

I see my sunsets as yesterday's
Fond childhood memories closely wove—
Toys, sweets, dreams, wars, words,
All playing to sandman whims
Into one great big patched patchwork quilt
Covering noneties in ill-graced maze.

I see my sunsets as yesterday's
Grown-upped disregard for safer things
Mellowed ofttimes not by childhood sweets
Grown, grown much too soon, this antelope
Scribed in orphaned singular acrostic.

THE TICK OF THE FALLS

It's nice to visit the folks back home
To feel the tie that binds friendship's harp
For no matter where these bones make roam,
There're hearts in keep those secrets sharp
In wait another visit back home.

The years make rage the facial age,
But memory grows the stronger in thirst a face
Childhood told friendship's sage;
Oh, there's always in those hearts a place
When a visit makes nice the folks back home.

The buildings may have aged,
Some lives may have raged,
But friendship writes a book many paged
Ever in loose a soul that's encaged
When a visit and friends become engaged
To memories only a visit can bring
Beside the tick of the falls.

A MAGIC BEHELD

The desires of heart stronger than life itself
and pungent the pull by horse of day.
If there be the grieved, the grieved grieves to self
on this wagon pulled out of the streams of way
by the riders holding the heart of self.
Though pulled by sorrow, joy holds to its
sway of desires in heart stronger than life itself.

The desires of the heart, though reaching the unknown,
most pungent herb cannot their throbs delay,
and sweeter be the plains of the unknown
when the pull by the horse of day will relay
to elves with trinkets claiming the unknown
with cloven wands that sprinkle no betray
to the desires of heart seeking the unknown.

Soon must desires of heart give to life itself,
and wagon pulled by horse of day must stop
to feel the shake of hand in friend of self.
Lest there be in heart a ruined and sterile crop,
none but the vain would barter of itself;
there shall be those dreams the heart would not drop
as desires of heart have strengthened life itself.

AND DAY MUST BEGIN

Sun is spawning fingerling of day;
Chill of night is warmed by fiery beams.
Sister sun's golden hair's at play,
Sewing shadows with golden seams.
Thoughts burst in a moment's desire
And bloom on a kite string to and fro.
The height of will begins respire,
Singing its song with the morning's glow.
Dew of the mind weighs the grasses bent
Towards a goal on web just begun;
Spider of will grasps the moth's nonrepent
And flings hope to desires' rising sun.
The herald of nature chases defeat;
Violets fumble lenten path—
For there be no regret and no retreat
In the promise of the sun's first laugh.

SITTING HIGH ON THE SEAZT

Watch out!
      Old four-wheeler's on the road,
Looking like a reproducing toad,
Wide wheels
      and air shocks to the limit;
If he'd figure a way to shim it,
Those eighteen-wheelers
      would look like toys––
WATCH OUT!
      He's going into a curve, boys!

Hearing him
      in a beer joint one day,
You'd think Paul Bunyan had the highway;
He bragged about
      all those two-wheelers
He yanked
      from ditch like Pittsburgh Steelers––
Come to think of it, I like their help,
But on my rear they leave me a whelp.
An' now I'm sitting high on the seazt.

I'm sitting high on the seazt, boys;
I'm sitting high on the seazt,
Breathing no bad gas—no sweets.
I'm sitting high on the seazt, boys;
I'm riding high on the seazt,
Wheeling my wheeler on the streets.

SAY-SOS

Why is it peoples from oldest antiquity to present time
have heard themselves and their leaders so often say so
that the world is better even day after day? Why is it?
It is either that words are shouted into a bottomless
canyon, where their echoes are never turned to glance the
searching ear, or the world was millions of times worst
than today's worst worst. Count it, my friend, count it.

Why are these only words? Where are those displays gone
shouting, proving the best of better and the worst that
was, when all are hang gliding between other troublesome
mountain? One moment a soul can be hanging on to heaven's
gate. The next moment shins the tar on to Hell Eblis;
then comes a moment in apologies, and middle roads gleam.

Can it be that yesterday's better is today's worst and
tomorrow's ever in battle which time it was that passed
in dig the well through this body of clay, echoing not
in each better canyon? Where is the better? Say so, say!
How is it that better stands still? How tells the worst
when worst is a triumph for another birth? Why? Why's it
that a coffin must be unearthed before the shout's heard.
"Better and worst are not here?" Prove it, my ego friend!
Prove it in your heart! It dies on the lips then floats
in the wind, but worst is worst when no one hears.

FAMINE'S QUILTING BEE

Famine quilts herself a dream
     with patches of meadow parch
And stitches with cartilage
     flies have cleaned of carrion.
She calls her design
     Temples of the Dead.

The lining is of burial shrouds,
Dens and lairs of death-stalked hunger,
where dust and moths tint the fabric
with a touch of pollen in memory of life
as a God home-calls the quilters
to a festival of prodigal souls.

The quilting seams recall the boundaries
of corals once jovial to life's floods,
and those cries and moans and tears
done in helplessness incense the biers
pall-borne in hearts far removed from scene
to bless with votive light in Temples of the Dead.

Famine quilts the road and sings her song:
Rebirth of life looks through windows long,
But can a word call famine's quilt right or wrong?

BEFORE WAR CRIES

*There are still barbarians in the world who set the price for
peace at death or enslavement and the price is too high.*

—Ronald Reagan, Sept. 15, 1972

If brothers cannot abide
      in the cloth of blood
Succored by love of mothertide,
Are we destined in pools of mud
      to laugh at others cried?

Impatience is a thrusting sword,
      denying tongue a brain bath,
Which knocks the bones on toward
      a division of its jungled path,
Switching to a leaf not so bored.

Are all the wars ever raged
      and all the words ever pitched
But connect of nothing to nothing gagged
Through the ply of ego witched
      for a place in the sun so caged?

To some, war is kids at a Chinese festival
Excited by noise and brilliant light,
Thinking nothing more so festive
Than to calm the nerves with noisy sight
And shout the air become restive dull.

GODS AND MOUNTAINS

There is something about a mountain
All the gods have been enamored to
Up in the heights, gathering and accounting
The times they've sent their sweetest due.

On a mountain the halo of the gods can be seen
In waterfalls drinking rainbows
With spray of holiness in brightest sheen,
Splashing wisdom upon our woes.

All the living have gone up mountains
To wrestle with their visions planned
And study in their gall and mountings
To grind the rock of vision into sand.

There are some in lose their mountain,
Others scale there one or two,
But hopes live in water of fountain
When a mountain is reasoned through.

THE PRICE OF GLUTTONY

I looked upon a finger towel
And said, "I, I thought more dined than me."
The diner said with burp from bowel,
"Oh, pardon my lack of poverty."
He took another from its dowel
And covered his lap so politely.
He gave to me his finger towel
And said, "I, I thought more dined than me."
Then all my dinner came from bowel
And pooled into my towel on knee.
The diner looked and frowned as he growled,
"Suppose we'll blame it on gluttony."
He took from lap his cleaner towel
And offered other on plate to me.
The dog that's beneath the table howled
To think I more hungry than he.
The dog's tail tucked and away he yowled;
He never would eat of dine so free.
The diner took my plated towel
And ate at the table haughtily.

OH PEACE, GIFT ME

There was a tree beside a cave,
Where sat a thinking thoughtful knave
Looking at a star away, far,
Reverberating light afar,
Reminding him of darkened way,
Distanced of light in cave's bright ray.

He thought a message smiled at him:
Why sat he beneath and between
A darkened night and light's bright beam?
Why not seek the message heralded,
Could goody good be beamed, unfurled,
To a knave come dreaming at night
Beneath a tree's all-speckled light?
But must he go, his life was caught
As a leaf so tangled in thought.

Then a voice came smiling on ear:
Why stake out life on sorrow's tear?
Then staking thought emerged in light;
He followed fear's so awesome fright
And stood a-gaze at crib in cave.
His quickened heart, a gift it gave.

DAISY LAND

I pulled a daisy
Eating dirt,
Smiling back at sun,
Doing battle game
At shiny mirror
Hung on dewy balls.

A cricket
Spies her mate
Playing hide-and-seek
At Daisy's toes,
Dancing in chirruped song
As cricket files her bones.

Cricket who espied
To matey cricket
Rushes her hovel door
Unhinged at bottom sling
For air-conditioned space.

The space so tiny grooved
Dissipated
Male cricket's ego,
Disdained by singing cricket
Peeking through dewy panes,
Growing small in shine of sun,
Galloping onward in sky
Chased by nimble clouds
About to shed their tears
On Daisy, cricket, and I.

Daisy Susan stared at me
For doing crazy thing;
I pulled
Her whitened hair
As whispering my love song:
She loves me, she loves me not.
Oh, Daisy, why can't you
Grow one more hair?

MY CAMPFIRE FRIEND

With head bowed in friendship's press,
I spin my web encircled within
Friendship's new moon
Orbiting round warm stars in spark,
Twinkling, enlightened, enthroned
'Pon essayed bliss.

Twinkle my stars
In heaven's clear sea,
Burn 'til words fathomed ship
Burst its doors in watery spurn.
Heap tirades of nerves' enjoy
On this friendship's bright flame.

Shushed in while, gypsy's mash
Brightens yawning hour;
I cast heather's sweet bane
O'er my spun web enflamed,
Indeed enflamed, to smiles' wispy sprite
E'er watchful to coals' ebbing sight
Whitened once and only
In hypnotic, entrancing plane.

Embers die but once:
My friendshipping love
Dies heartily, slowly,
In hearts my embers touch,
Touched in my embered flame.

LOCKED WITHIN OURSELVES

We trolley our wares
To others' appeal
Ripened in their dares
To fortune's wheel.

We trolley our wares
Not in weather's vane,
Just heaping our cares
Down servient lane.

Our wares we trolley,
Though loved by self,
Fall to others as folly
Down that road called delft.

Our wares thus trolleyed
Oft break much-loaded shelf
By failure's voice hollied
Thousand times o'er
By past wisdomed cleft,
Crying, crying through paneled door,
Locked in one's own self
As stranger from without
Shouts: the blind need door no more.

THE RAFFLER'S WAY

Scavengers
Ate my heart away,
Clothed in friendship,
Suited to suit of gray,
Preying,
Preying upon emotions' way
In sing their song,
All is fair play.

Gracious words
Tremble their lips of clay,
Threshing,
Threshing the chaff of day.

Rolling tongue,
Moving their air
O'er wills who may
Grasp the tarnish
Burning as some bright ray.

Turning,
Turning wheel of carded bin
In select predestined
For some baubled ride.

Losers,
Losers in ever cry,
Shout their feelings
Into vats of rye,
Never,
Never keep the peeling
For pockets' jingle, nigh.

TRAIL MY HORSE

Trail my horse
To the bloody ride;
Let the sage sing my song,
Tumbling on, tumbling on,
Plucking strings of daiseylins
Conchoed by rattletars.

My trail, though short or e'er long,
Leaves the beaten path
In my quest for life's sure song
Etched in dusty dunes
By horseman and hooves.

Trail my horse
Through countryside so tranquil;
There I'll ply my soulful needs
'Til the bloody ride
Ends in city's nonplussed deeds
Done in glow of eventide.

Trail my horse
In wait of each new ride;
I've no done thus deed
I'd quite willful hide.
Me, my trail, and horse,
Born to freedom's wind,
Just gallops off
To others seen-thus sin.

Trail my horse
To the bloody ride;
Ask the sage tumbling on,
Striking at my new past dune,
"Where's the horseman
Just rode by
In lonely he knows tune?"

Trail my horse
I'll gladly ride
O'er much-trod trail;
I'll see all old ways
In freedom's wind
Just torch of past smoothed bends
In memories' lane.

Bloody scorched my ride
With human wants.
Trail my horse
In bridled desires.
Spur my steed
O'er wanton's pile.
Stagger my horse
In smiles' last mile.

So trail my horse
And let me ride
'Pon freedom's wind
Born each day anew.

RACING HYMN

A planter told to me
Some dreams
I've never dreamt:
How asparagus
So quickly grows
In restful
Days of spring,
Drinking wells
Of vitamins,
Shooting bullets
Straight and tall;
Just pick a few
With knifing blades all sharp—
E'en asparagus
Fears bite and bark.

How beans poled
And beans bushed
Same race
With different-head hair.
Breaking open
Long green pod
Of beans poled
And beans bushed
Retold to me
The aged man's tale:
To children
Race is only one;
Grown-ups take accidents'
Opine as happen to them
And mix dark,

Dark brewed teas
To rot the fruitful
Fruit of reason.

Told me how berries
Grow on vine and bush:
Blackberries,
Raspberries,
Plenty 'xamples be;
Vine will crowd the bush
Absent long
From the pruner's hook
Though flesh of same mien.

TASSELED

Come to my warming
Not with smiles or cries.
Bring me not your smile's
Worn and frayed lip balm.
Drop not your tears
'Pon my discordant palm
Clutched in fear many years.

Let not my warming
Hassle your indie charms.
Smiles and laughter,
Wrinkles and frowns,
Cries or tears,
Early breaks this warming
If from hearts
They bleed sincere.

THE KNOCK

A stranger came to my door
without bell, bottle, or song;
I stood in the door
and drank in this friendship long.
I heard the tones of a distant bell
reflecting me in this clear, still well.
I was bottled all up as opaque light
until the stranger gave me sight;
so dumb was I, I broke into song
as the stranger went his way along.

THE OAK AND POISON IVIES

Of all the plants in the kingdom wild,
There is a vine of juice not mild,
Rambling on in viny style
To lick the flesh of even child.

Trinity is its deviled leaf
Itching the flesh with blistered grief
That only time can bring relief
To the brush by vine so brief.

All of those to the woodland's know
Shy the tree up which it's grown
Until the winter bare its bone
When the cardinal near has flown
To pluck its seed for otherwhere sown.

When the oak and poison ivies
Wrap my longing heart in grief,
There is none, none to sigh relief
To this trembling, dying leaf
Passing life into eternity, brief.

DEBATE

'Mongst the threads and bares of human tears,
The Jimson grows to skyward heights
With trumpet pure and bright,
In beckon all ineptitudes.

The orchestrated spines
In orb the Jimson weed
Frights the highing ones
To fitful, childish games.

Fingering those moments of requite,
The low ones break that orb
Encircling the Jimson weed,
Finding poison's need of hide.

Come taste the highing exercise
Doped with syllabicated words
Contained beneath one Jimson seed
Dressed in foolery's hardened case.

Come, share the contested fest
Dueling in goodwill's stead,
Feeding the fruits of centuries' bane
Into a nation's o'erdrunk ball.

Come, reason, inhabit the coop
Once more in need the chaff from floor;
Sing that song of deliverance once more,
The peoples come to clear the floor.

The droppings haste
The kiss of floor to ceil,
Shall the twain in embrace be met
Through the windows of fear
Whilst truth holds open the door.

Debate, my friend,
'Til whirlwinds cease
Their rape of natured things,
'Til maws grow closed
In truth's healing salve,
'Til words both read and heard
Lose their pith of mean.

THE PICTURE ON MY WALL

In glowering,
A picture hangs upon my wall,
Its silence beckons goodly mail.
Awaked am I in scene so small
As eye in travel sees a pail
All dappled red with sandy scrawl,
Unwinding for me, the sea's remissive tale,
Consuming waves' hypnotic call,
Devouring things without fail,
Those redauntless versions feared by all.
Would they demurely hail
In crashing terrestrial fall
As beaching beggars trenching trail
On sacred bed of Wavipaw,
Imbued to glassy veil
Of thousand legions standing tall,
Fire their guns in hopeful whipping rail,
Removing trespass, breaching mall?
Billowed waves unfurl each sail
And cover greatly in sounding drawl
A picture's red and sandy pail,
Shying shovel's weighty mail
As my eyes in sleep doth fall,
Wondering tale
Of my picture on wall.

TARNISHED SHORES

Spill o'er harshly, ye waterfalls,
Burst open dam containing thy force.
Free thy fish and other water calls.
Empty thy unious soul
Till voice grows quite hoarse.
Let waves from tongue roll.

Forget but self,
It too must swell with rain
Till jaws in pain doth cleft
From thoughts thus seemed not sane,
Swilling round yon bend.

Thy journey, seaward bent,
Ebbs long fore home once seen
As rapids calm thy wrathful repent
And riplets split thy spleen.

Rejoice aft gainly falls
As elsewhere's baths the mermaid;
She, too, in love recalls
Her home and tarnished shores.

BEHIND THE EUCHARIST

I'm Christopher Fox
On the way to God's
    own locks,
Where the flooding stream
Stops at self-esteem;
I'm the ruler, sure,
Of my soul's endure,
Drinking waters, pure,
From God's own grandeur.

My Savior surely
Gave a gift truly
In the bread purely,
In the wine's true blood
To me, at the locks
Stopping time's own clocks
While I, Christopher,
Let God rule my life.

God's on the altar;
Why should I falter
When God's part of me,
Making me so free?

He's friend come to me,
A friend I can't see;
How lovely to talk
Without any chalk
Between Christ and me.

I draw a picture
Of Jesus in mind;
He dwells in my heart,
I live with his love,
I can shape the world
God's living in me.

CARRIAGE, MANNER, AND DEMEANOR

Come out of the rain, my son,
The stepping-stones are wetted
with tears;
Once I built my house
In the forest cleared by faith,
But others held
      the nostalgic door
And took a stepping-stone
To grace their house of fears.

If two millennia seem
      as a day to you,
Thanks for bringing
      the stepping-stone
Closer to the altar, in dew;
My stepping-stone
Is not placemark for bone.
The dead frequent not
      my place of chew;
Come out of the rain, my son,
Bring the stepping-stone
with you.

Beside my stepping-stone path,
Some say there grows a weed,
But each soul must
      share a laugh
Before another finger
can lead
The stepping-stone
      missing its path;
Come out of the rain, my son,
And dry my path of tears.

If my missing stepping-stone
Shines not of faithful greed,
Surely the moss o'ergrown
      the hole
Shall cease when stones
gathered in place;
My path shan't look as bold
When all's in share my grace.
Come, let the stepping-stones
Hold the meaning to my place.

Do not all stepping-stone paths
Stop at every door?
Have I not one day said,
He who is not against is for
My way devoid of bore?
So, husband,
      my missing stepping-stone,
It announces the visit
      coming a day before.

Come out of the rain, my son,
The stepping-stones
        are yet wet with tears,
Each body must have its fun
Before my door opens
to cheers;
If each would bring
        his stepping-stone
Next to pathway's end,
No longer
        would we cry for bone
For joy would have
        an unceasing crescendo.

Come onto
        my stepping-stone way,
The stones dry their tears,
The sweeper tills the day,
The dirt has flown away;
No need for a stepping,
        Stepping-stone way,
There's a task, not a bull,
To at our hearts pull.
Does not a stepping-stone way
End at
        the cornerstone's sway?

FADS A-CHANGING

Where are the noble,
The quick,
The brave?
Gone, gone to the grave.

Where are the kind,
The genteel,
The sane?
Gone, gone in exile's row.

Where are the aged,
The aborted,
The grassers indeed?
Gone, gone to the scalpel's song.

Where are the rulers,
The kings,
The queens?
Gone, gone to ghetto's street.

Where are the gods,
Their laws,
Their means?
Cut down, cut down by the one.

Where are the people,
The bag holders,
The goats of scape?
Gone, gone to love's open gate.

OUTDONE

'Twill be in the will,
'Twill be in the will,
'Twill be in the will.
Little Bill,
'Twill be in the will.

Don't kill me, little Bill,
Don't kill me.
'Twill be in the will.

Wait, little Bill;
Don't kill me, little Bill.
'Twill be in the will.

Interest grows in the will,
Little Bill,
Interest grows in the will.

You're too young, Papa Bill,
You're too young.
Got to kill you, Papa Bill;
Can't wait for the will.

Die brave, Papa Bill,
Die brave for your son, Bill.
Got to have that will,
Papa Bill.

Papa Bill's dead, Judge Will,
Papa Bill's dead.
Where's the will, Judge Will?
Where's the will?
Papa Bill said, Judge Will,
'Twill all be in the will.

Sonny Bill cries, Judge Will,
Sonny Bill cries,
Reading Papa Bill's will;
'Tis all in the will.

Papa Bill wills, Judge Will,
Papa Bill wills.
All to courthouse seal.
Papa Bill says son kills,
Judge Will.
'Tis all in the will.

Sonny Bill, I, Judge Will,
Sentence you to lifelong years.
Papa Bill wills;
'Tis here in Papa Bill's will.

A COWARD LENDS HIS GRACE

Behind these walls, I take refuge
From mental tasks and attitude,
Bathe myself in public monies
Given without court's fight.
Peasants are such a gentle clan,
Showering king in worshipland.

To my peasant I would say:
Must wars be fought
With others' blood,
Feigning a coward's o'erchewed cud?
As gentle peasants pay the tax
For foundation's wick,
Their own flesh becomes the wax
Consumed in a coward's trick.

National interest, the sulphuric flame,
Ignites the public wick.
Gentle peasants in sentenced blame
Metered in battle's quick
And desperate control of man;
'Tis the smothering coward's fan,
His burning weapon always pans.

Walk my way, you brave to eyes.
See my mind, the hero's room.
Drape my cloth o'er court's chair;
'Tis I chasing bag of lies
To hero's lion's share.

WORMWOOD

Man must have his women,
Man must have his wine,
Man must have his given
Chorus to flute
His discordant rhyme.

He does within his world
Paint his bright, sunken moat
With himself in the sails, furled
'Pon ships of other coat.

TOUCH OF MADNESS

There are ways.
There are means.
He behaves
In his dreams.

Dreams bring dread,
Dreams bring smiles,
Only in bed
Feet steal miles.

Miles are inches,
Miles are long,
Miles go trenches
In everyday song.

Song is mirth,
Song is sad,
Song has worth
Though tune goes mad.

Mad my eyes,
Glad my heart,
Body cries
Pierced by dart.

Darts are sharp,
Darts are dull,
Mind asks harp
Vibrate skull.

Skulls are wise,
Skulls are dumb,
All surmise
Their own plum.

Plums are sweet,
Plums are bitter,
With discreet
We should twitter.

TEDI BARS

To the city gone,
Gone from cropping rows,
Gone from teddy bores
To city skyward grown.

To the city gone,
Pitching pennies to hungry mouths;
No pennies left
To lavish humanity's boughs.

Gone from cropping rows
To city's mingled charms,
The lowly weeds in their knows
Shade our paths grown in qualms.

Gone from teedy bores
To city's bricked-up shine,
Left behind a gen of mores
In search of full body o'mine.

Gone to city skyward grown
As trees in forest of home
But void of boughs windway mourns,
Shunted by piercing bird of siren.

Hungry mouths loathe penny shine
Far from hearty warmth
Of cropping rows' clime
Traded for great city's moment glow.

To the city gone,
Lacking know of farm;
'Tis in lately bosom's lode
We find faith in cropping rows.

Look to the city
For your fair lain delights;
Sun may not strike your doorpost,
Nor moon seen 'pon your nights.

Look to the city
As someday has said
City makes sinners, saints indeed,
City makes saints, sinners decreed.

Look to the city
For bus, gongs, and sounds
Wheeled to fortune's tell,
Just each making his rounds
'Pon the cropping rows.

BALLAD OF THE RACE

The race is o'er,
The battle begun,
Wagon 'fore the horse—
Some farmer outdone.

Seeded furrows covered just deep;
Mystery remains
Till earth cracks from sleep.

(Voter)
One curtain baring two feet;
Sower plants his seed
'Tween mystery of a sheet.

(Vote influence)
In obey of freedom's watered need,
Essence trembles
In trumpets' soundless beat.

(Apathy)
One vote, though the cup o'erflow;
Not my fault
But fault of cup's mini show.

(Delinquent voter)
One booth
In silent draped open poll
Yelled in silent public eye.

(Delinquent voter attitude)
One nonsower
Failed the furrow fall.
One seed failed to die,
Not worthy e'en the hod;
Yet und shelves' dusty crust
Away from verse of trusty bard,
One nonsower shouts his lust:
My vote
Shan't sweeten corrupt musts.

(Tellers)
The gathers
Of rooted seedling bed
Count the leaves
Of seeded furrow;
Mystery solved but not yet wed
In time of song to sparrow.

(Vote analysis)
As farmer reasons
His sparse grown rows,
Senses his furrow thrown
'Pon seed of other times grows,
Late in dress for naked bone,
All is harvest but few alone.

SWEET PILLOW OF DOWN

'Round yon huddle
Of gossip-free love
Stands the stillness of death
'Til whispers ruffle a string
Tuned in nonreaching pitch
High o'er the bastion of mind,
Low to frailty unkempt.

Passersby throw an unleavened eye
To children of gossip-free love
Frenzied in wallow mire,
Tending garden of nonbloom
Grown o'er by weedy speech:
How's my love
To slither in belly dance
With heart chasing the moon?

A dove flies o'er
This gossip-free love ring,
Stayed by sipping of love
In friendship's nonfriendly song,
Chasing morals after dying dove.

This dove circles ne'er more
Gossip-free love's sing:
How's my love
To slither in belly dance
With heart chasing the moon?

I walk on by
In simple-songed refrain
Past gossip-free love's ring.
I no longer run in reign
Of mortal love's putrid ting-a-ling.
I've placed my score
On higher-sounding board
To die in gossip-free love no more,
Watching love freely outpoured.

My simple-songed refrain
Scatters the huddled remain;
I've donned that cheating cloth
Till life parts to other train
And head laid fore'er in loft
Of grave's sweet pillow of down.

SIGHT UNSEEN

He sees the moon
and sets the force's pull
'til eons cease the work,
but oh, does he see me?

He sees the stars
bobbing in galaxies afar;
I wonder, I wonder,
oh, does he see me?

He hides in the clouds,
the squirming billowry clouds,
silvery, shimmering now,
growing threateningly dark,
but oh, does he see me?

He dresses the fields
in weed and flowered bloom
as they bless the plan,
but oh, does he see me?

He sends a blessed grace
o'er this creatured mind
in grope the lesson be,
but oh, does he see me?

He blows his wind,
sweet sweeper of chaff,
in clear the question be
o'er this troubled mind.

He kisses the thoughts
of my current flow,
echoing in whispered glee—
yes, o yes, he does see me.

He sends and hides,
he sees and dresses
all thoughts in hide of him,
oh great sight unseen.

THE FEEL OF THE ROAD

I went looking for joy one day
along the arbored country lane,
whose air was crisp,
whose freshness could be seen;
My soul was bubbling with joy,
all joyed to country lane.

My joy quaked a bit
for hidden in the shadowy brush
two bodies close I saw.
My stance in lane, I stood
as crippled thought glanced my brow
whilst trembling bodies flew the scene.
"Is this joy?" I asked my soul
with me in this arbored country lane.

Once again my walk I begun
along this arbored country lane,
whose air was crisp,
whose freshness could be seen.
My song to soul hung in note
as the bird flew its bush.
One body aloft in fruited tree
jumped to ground.
Its hidden face could not be seen
though apples garlanded its wake.
"Is this joy in joy's ambush?"
I again asked my soul.

I must not stop my search;
no, not just now
in this arbored country lane,
whose air was crisp,
whose freshness could be seen,
bids me on
abiding the mingled search of mean.

I sat upon one thinking bench
and quietly listened
to a pair long time had not seen;
their speech weighed heavily
upon other's faults not known,
this laughing noise
found me no restful while.

I sauntered on down
the arbored country lane,
whose air was crisper,
whose freshness felt and seen.

Boisterous cries
split the freshness from crispy air
as hayriders came close to me;
their sensuous cursing chords
made laughter seem as a joke.
I asked my searching soul,
"Is this the joy of my search?"
It's nonreply not heard by me
Quickened my steps in lane.

The scene I saw
at end of this country lane,
whose air was crisp,
whose freshness felt and seen,
put the joy back into my soul.
I saw a father and mother,
a sister and brother,
beginning their walk with me
back on down the arbored country lane,
whose air was fresh,
whose crispness felt and seen,
through the joy
of this foursome gleam.

FOLKS AND BIBLE TALK

Oh, if folks had not habits,
there'd be no Bible at all;
'twould be but the sages of man
dusting the troubadour's quiet refrain.

But folks do have habits,
small and big, good and bad,
whose judge in nonretirement
quotes in Bible talk
to folks in seem much more sad.

Folks and Bible talk
mix the sage with the mace,
brew their own conjurations
in fit the need to finish race
to prove the better fixation.

THE MEASURE

Linger, my child,
In words' daily play,
List each syllable
Flowing o'er the heart.

Ponder, my child,
The mean of each word
Thrown to gale wind,
Ever o'er the pits,
In speak to opti-land.

Gather, my child,
The fruit from chaff,
'Tis the heart, not the word,
Flowing to character made.

Hast you grown from child
To man of statued means,
By this measure cup,
As others measure you.

ANVIL FORCE

Fit as an axe,
But axe won't fit
Upon this tree of mine,
Tempered by public force
Askance in private while.

The tree grown much too long
By the swamp of endeavor's child
Chastised not by mental whipsichord
In wait, more opportune time,
Late, if ever on timbered flesh.

The bleeding tree of retrospect
Heals its wound in never time
As resin flows to public force,
And the anvil grows cold by fire
As embers die in private while.

Too-chee, too-chee, too-chee,
Rings the hammer in steady blow
O'er the cold still-willed mind
As public force tempers the heart
And breaks the nettled private while.

THE PEEK

The baby lies in crib.
The baby-teaching guardian
Lies his beguiling crib,
Telling giant come for peek,
This the way of love.

The giant, in nonwhimsical mood,
Lifts his brow to thoughts,
Thoughts in mild platitudes,
He sees himself in mirrored face
Just born to self anew.

UNDER THE COLUMBINES

Under the columbines
And through the wetted dew,
We pitch our thoughted minds
To the grand subdued view.

Over the greening covered reaches,
Our lazy thoughts scramble the leaves
As nodding heads to welcome speeches
Smile the hare in stomach achieves.

Daiseytoes in cry some stealthy hands,
In pick its brightened head and blushing face,
Sings its song to rustler fans
Come with good germ in wedded grace.

Under the columbines
And through the wetted dew,
Our souls in rejoice o'er reserpine
Whistles a tune in natured revue.

Hear the bee in steadied whine
Stop the moments o'er perfumery's place
As transparent wings in smell the triune vine,
Rape the virgin of clover's race.

Under the columbine
And through the wetted dew,
Know you now why the columbine
In mimicry clover dress, like new,
Carries the spurs like briary vine
In wanton not her wallflower
Some hasty, lazy bee to chase in subdue.

271

Suffer my feet on other lands to trod.
Feast my eyes on endeavors' plains.
Nimble my hand o'er the clovered reach
As speaks my tongue to eon's ring.

Trod those lands of unsearched heart;
Under the columbine and wetted dew,
Find that egg removed from path.
Pick those stones unlept by hand.
Tell the heart of creation's find.

Those lands of trod, unknown.
That egg watched, unbirthed.
The hand by clover, untouched,
Yet my tongue vibrates the praise
Under the columbines
And through the wetted dews.

FROM PROMISE TO PROMISE

I've rocked in the chair, creaking,
And found my mind gone a-hunting,
O'er the hills and vales a-seeking
The promise of life at sunrise,
Blinking to natured dreams.

I've sat my chair, straight,
Waving to reasoned train
Crossing rivers gone to mate,
The sea with toggle,
Thought and minnioned main.

I've lain in chair, plush,
Watching minutes weigh the hours
As sparrows crowd and break the bush,
Waking me in my bed of flowers
'Fore this body dies by mental crush
And spirits-like petal fall
Cov' me o'er under their bower.

I've sat my chairs, all,
And in momented disgust
Shy the covers for a shawl,
Leaving those chairs of distrust,
And go back in life squall
To rock in that chair, a-creaking,
To the promise of life at sunrise,
Leaping from promise to promise.

FROWNS, FRETS, AND SMILES

Oh, countenance, steering a load,
Stirring humanity's emotion swing
Pushed to and fro by sway of node
As each flirts his bird on wing.

Oh, countenance, o'ergrown the world,
Plying sweet-shadowed smiles
To cart humanity hurled
Forth for a change in styles.

Oh, countenance, debtor of styles,
Crawling 'neath that cart hurled
Cringing those wheels stealing that smile
From the cloth of opinion, unfurled,
To smiles gone a-chasing
Frets and frowns on life's turnstile.

WET COBBLESTONES

I go 'mongst the tears,
'Mongst silver and gold
Icons of age just past,
Mingled in dusty fingerprints old,
To say, well, I'm not the last
Tolling the bell as told.

I go 'mongst the tears
To read these memoried lines
As mind message adheres
To all mingled climes,
In mirrored reflections,
Told by our past lives
As past to present o'ershines
Future's sense cud,
That taste of touch,
Dampens somewhat
Our ebullient drives,
Thinking not future
Only our past as such;
Though once known, profits us much.

I go 'mongst the tears
Possessed by five senses, small,
Hearing the woodwinds—
Their faint forestry call.
Smelling the pine
O'erheat by kindly sun.
Seeing its needles green
Then fall to earth
In patchwork yet not done.

Touched its many-seamed trouser leg.
Felt its burnished pallet
With nosey barefoot toe.
Sensed its eternal cycle of beg,
Naked arms aching to grow.
Tasted pungent oils of energy cells,
Its tale told not
By each ringing of the bells.

I go 'mongst the tears
When self is known
With virtues not o'ergrown;
When the triplets of time
Make a life beautiful in rhyme.
'Tis then I go 'mongst the tears,
Carrying not a pocket burden,
That soiled handkerchief,
With tale of life uncertain.
Then 'tis true of my leaf,
I walk tearfully 'mongst the tears.

HORIZONS AT PLAY

Oh, great forested horizon
Swaying in the gentle breeze,
Chattering to unseen, unknown stars
As they wink in spastic delight.

Oh, great horizon,
Like as frest mown meadow grass
In welcome of the small creatures
Lessening their labored trot.

Oh, great forested horizon,
Great impenetrable distant screen,
Giving mind its sight of discovery
In wondered thought,
Has other side eyes have seen.

Oh, great forested horizon,
Imagery's lesson long, long viewed
As mountains and castles,
Hovels and vast wheaten plains,
Give our lazy moments,
That praise, that praise past due.

Oh, great forested horizon,
Long in wait the marriage to sky,
Call you the raven, the gull,
All birds of flapping wings,
Rustle the message bugles love to cry.

Oh, great forested horizon,
Let all battles begin and die,
All quarrels and sins done in the rye
Rest once and e're in the eye.

Oh, great forested horizon
Jealous of sunrise and sunset,
Envious of moon fully dressed
Lest we forget the dappled shade.

Oh, great forested horizon
Hiding rainbow's fall to earth,
Beckoning lightning's frightful sword,
Giving humans view that courage of friend.

Oh, great forested horizon,
This good earth's holder and pulchritude,
Unkind chasms and zealous swamplands
Hold no great labor nor grieve to you.

Oh, great forested horizon
In tell a nation's mind and heart,
Tell all peoples thy secret held
Neath that centuried veil of wisdom stored.

Oh, horizon framed by forestkind,
Wouldst thy star, sun, and stealthy moon,
Lightnings, clouds, and cometed tails,
Look as good without the forest hide.

Oh, great forested horizon,
Your song to mind does sing:
Pictures in the forest,
Oh, pictures live and green,
Picture of the dead and not so lively seen.
Pictures, pictures, pictures,
Pictures not painted;
Oh, what high esteem.

SPEAK, SHAKE, AND ROLL

Move, you sloven one, move
In life's boiling stew,
Speak your foaming tongue,
Though 'tis only through bitter lips.

Shake your head, cloven,
To neck's weak-pinned sinew,
Glare those seething eyes
To stalled one in race.
Shake your finger all
Though crooked in own ways.

Roll those sleeves
To elbow's plain,
Strike at the souling base
Sieved in truth's knot sane.

Speak, shake, and roll
In life's boiling stew;
Speak, shake, and roll
That foaming tongue
Though 'tis moved in true.

FIVE ELEMENTS OF LEARN

Water, moon fire, and song
Breaks our mooding, brooding heart
When hid from view too soon or long
By earth's pulling curtain smart
'Gainst naked tide's tong-sure.

Water, water, great barrier reef
In sing of our commote
Lashing our heart in relief
Aft carrying loads' great tote,
Sighing, almost dying in grief.

Moon the great gripper,
Grasping our singing heartstrings
Thrown to love's great dipper
O'er loaded in noneties' brings
Given once more to other sipper.

Fire, fire, smoking, flaming fire,
Blinding our eyes now enflamed
To arms and lips enmeshed as wire
Molten in hearts gamed
Elsewhere, for moments' liar.

Melody makes not our gaming psalm
Noted and pitched as symphony
Running on to last alarm.
Melody cares not the harm,
Just its moments in lyrical bliss.

There's water, moon, fire, and song
Dancing cross our paths grown long;
Stoop, bend, pick, and kiss
Your blossom of pitched thong.

TO CHORUS SUNG

Oh, you quaker of menial tasks,
Grind those dingy teeth.
Point that shaking bone
To me, the beast of burden's abode.

Smile that faking, stenching breath
When smile's the price of secrecy torn
From fainting lips of union's child
Come from meet,
Whose tale is as still as death.

Frown, you quaker of menial talks,
Best be true to station's berth
Than in think a smile's the price
In purchase a union's true red blood.

A CRIB IS ALL

I'll find my God
In the blessed marriage bed,
Away from the chides of life
And quarrels bad, bad fest.

I'll find my God
In the silent look of friend
As friend in look of me
Covers that hurt of soul.

I'll find my God
In the enemies' cresting cry
As they flay my flesh
But listen to words of soul.

I'll find my God
In all paths I walk,
Though the flower has died
But in wait its sow to grow.

I'll find my God
By the empty crib's call,
Calling to me, in search,
Is not a crib but all.

I'll find my God
Aft the blossom's faded
And this bode of gifted soul
Reaches out to afterlife.

WHOSE BUNTING

Wrapped in the clothes of cradle,
Rocked in the realms of deep,
Deep inebriating commune
As songed angel keeps wing
Wrapped 'round pillowed head
Attend to mind of God.

Two tiny feet in dream a-walking,
A-walking that ascending trial,
The trail to his mount of God
Splendored in lush meadowed green
Grown to timbres, envisioned
By cradled one seeing in sleep.

Two tiny hands, sculptured nice,
Waving hi and bye
To many friends enchoired,
Attuned to purity's nails.

TO WAYWARD PLACE

Children of flower tramping the flower bed,
Someone in other ranging thought
Grows for garland 'round their head,
Some poor, poor children bought.

Children of flower speaking the Jesus's name.
In common house of mental dime,
Singing hymns of passing the blame
From their covers to voted line.

Children of flower dancing in rags,
Denying inheritance house left in tears,
Though those tears leak the brags
To public eye grown fat on fears.

Children of flower dyeing love's store,
Wilting the flowers and munching the weed,
Telling tales mingled in satanic lore
Encircled 'round their selfish greed.

Children of flower speeding solitude's spin
Down windy chasm echoing single pitch
To fakery's unison mob glen,
Spading wide flowered death ditch.

Children of flower shouldering not gens' load,
Just lisping in syllabled nonday talk
As minions, wars, and strife-laden road
Gather the moss and forge freedom's stalk
To wayward place of cavernous gain.

THE TOLL OF THE DRUM

The last snowfall melts quickly by
To earth turning o'er in bed,
Wakening life sleep under white dye
As maple weeps in winged tear
Its show of life in bud—
Boom-ba, boom-ba, boom-ba boom.

The hare leaps forth, high,
In time of budding of the maple
As cat romps through the rye
To nature's beaten, espaliered tree
In the time of budding maple––
Ba-boom, ba-boom, boom, boom.

All wee birds on spastic wing
Dance called play of structured wind
In fortissimoed instinct come of age,
Though known not why natured secret kept
In this budding of the maple.
Ba-ba-ba-ba-ba-boom-ba, broom-broom, broom.

The mare, restless to swell of air,
Prances path long grown to weed,
Stops again with nostrils a-flare,
Paws the spot in want of knead
In the time of budding of the maple.
Ba-boom, boom-boom, ba-boom.

Long-slept bees uncrowd the hives
Though sweetened cupboard not very bare,
Nature tells the time arrives
For courtship of flowers in pretty hair
In the budding of the maple.
Ba-ba-ba-ba-boom-ba, boom-boom, boom-ba.

Hop on, you crazy hare;
Tear the dress, you flirting birds.
Knead the ground, you bucking mare;
Sip the nectar, you bees unheard
In this time of budding maple,
Growing dress for sheltering house.
Ba-ba-ba-boom-ba, boom, boom, boom-ba, boom.

All season's man dreads the maple bud,
Singing hymn of plowing song,
Drumming taps for onrushing sweat,
Keeping man from sweet easy chair
As maple hums its tune
In its time of maple bloom.
Boom, boom, boom, boom, boom.

Then, oh then, all season's man
Drapes his time long waited for
In purple mourning cloths
Hung 'til maple drops its bud
And drums beat more lilting hymn.
Baboom, baboom, baboom, baboom.

DEEP THE WOUND

Ever saw a wound
Deep by long by raw,
Closing eye too soon,
Phantom-thought faint?

Deep the wound of mind,
Long the years of heal,
Raw the scar remains,
Though friendship entwines
Deep by long by raw.

*****   ****   ****   ****

PURITAN'S SIN

Sunrise found you in pew
Religion studiously tended to.
Homeward bound for working clothes,
You've must work to do:
Cutting grass on Sunday,
Weeding garden same day,
Raking leaves in twilight,
Resting, drinking cold beer.
Playing cards Sunday night
To Penny Annie's delight.
Judging neighbor's nose down,
Peeping round page corner
Of *Playboy* magazine.
He comes not for visit
Nor beckons hi to you.
He wants meat
For his gossips stew.

****   ****   ****

GESTURED NOTE

Harped my chords to friend
On tuned instrument;
My friend sang me song,
Though not within tune.
I chorded on still
In perfect melody.

We looked each and grinned:
He sang perfect best.
I played perfect tune.

Who could have complained
In this perfect mansion
On compassion's hill?

SENTRIES CALL US

Roosters crow in the morning,
The lowly hiding cricket
Pumps in the day's work song,
Frogs croak in the night,
Katydids guarding realms about
Sentries each unknown bell,
We sleep in this rainbow
Of each well-guarded rite.

Why roosters crow
If not from fright?
Why crickets pomp
If not light too bright?
Why frogs croak
If not in their world uptight?
Why katydids sentry
If realm's all right?
Why we sleep
From flying our kite?

Roosters crow in
For want of mind.
Crickets pomp in
Seeing, hearing their kind.
Frogs croak in
Forgotten their grind.
We sleep in
Fore testing life's rind.

OH, DAY OF JOY

Christmas is a lovely time of year
Though ground's all froze
Or summer finds no end;
Yet the cock of love ever crows
In his flight of love, snuggling
To those who have grinned.

Christmas, one big holiday fest,
Divining hearts at friendshipping booths
Painted brightly in loving crest
Whichever beckons, ever soothes
That freedomed stag, fleeted.

Christmas on the greening heights,
Christmas in the valley low,
Christmas on the icy blights,
Christmas to ones of woe,
Christmas knows not place or clime,
Christmas shines on this heart-o-mine.

Christmas melting in the blow
Aft the presents, gifts, and wine,
After love's freckled doe
Has chased the dove a-flying
To Easter's resurrected snow.

Oh, day of joy
Flown much too soon
Into yesterday's
Pictured mental scene.

IN FLIGHT ONCE MORE

My joys fly elsewhere
Beyond this stubble earth
To realms of space long,
Long-thought bare,
In search of life and birth
E'er fleeing, voyaged trip,
So debonair.

My joys are I know not of;
Where's the slave
Who would die?
Where's barge, that bridge,
Low and above?
Other life, my sore,
I'll pass to renege.
I've not friendship,
That filling glove.

My joys fill my cup to o'erflow.
Why my waste in joy song
As sorrow fills my earth in sew
Of water splashing flesh in alarm.

I in flight once more
Glean the shepherd's purse
Bare of penny thoughts
'Til I in flight once more
Find the ghost of self.

CHAINS OF DUST

Today's child
Born to ransomed birth,
Why stain thy eye
With copious tear, so mild?

Today's child
Fondled in desire's bath
In water ne'er changed
Nor foamed in direction's path.

Today's child
In greet of empty home
Graced not by loving guardian
Gone e'er always
To pennies' snare.

Today's child
Fed bitter herbal fare
'Pon table of foster love,
Chasing God from marriage chair.

Today's child
Chained to mimicry
Throws his ankle ball
To break that mirror
Loved ones ply
To chains of rust.

WITH REGRETS AND ANGER

Yon Ethraim Fearshaker

Oh, hand-waving mobs throughout the world,
Bring down your skies to earth!
The world's on the brink
      with its crushing, rushing, race for arms!
Oh, cuss the tank of taxes
      given not for these alarms!
There's a devil in the house
      confusing rightful think
And laughing at the mob as a tiny holed-up mouse!

Oh, shouting peoples in the streets,
Lobby 'gainst the lobbyists' rule,
      making war out of peace!
And the poor man has not sweets
While the drums of nations drum their mournful beats!
And disease of human flesh spray the air
      with stenching wreaks!

Oh, gathering souls to savior-falling crowns,
Walk all day and run all night!
Push your prayers while none the others sleep!
Wake your leader while he's full awake!
Save the world for cause of waking's sake!

OH, PEACE

Peace is not dream, it's very real.
Sometimes it's truth one cannot feel
With fingers reaching for a crumb
But grasping not its sweetsome plum;
Still, there is the gift that's given
Strewn along the way that's driven
For you to seek its booty there,
A-giving something all can share.
It looks 'pon war as pride that's cleft
Away from man's more noble delft.
It sees all death as uncared sun
In honor not what peace has won;
Thus, peace is real and ever loved.
Let's give to peace what peace has loved.

WORRY NOT

In the seamless heights
Of society's bride,
Cometh worker's not,
Crying a loud cry:
'Tis an honor
To wallow in squalor
While others
Your staffs bear
Squalor 'tis only
Dastard states of mind.

Will and mind
Not gleaning talents lent
Nor treading ways inclement
To wandering, slothful ways,
Bearing the man's burden
Yet breaking his rod.
Groveling in treaty's brag
'Cause of much dunning
The honest man's bread.

Singing yon ballads,
Reeking of bestial acts
Planned to heroism
Whilst all along
Coverlets of pride,
Hiding present's glee.

Treaties gather not mold
Und threadbare feet,
Truly as the morrow,
State shall clothe thy bleat.

If every man
Could make his treaty,
Then treaties to the
Wind would bask.
'Twould not be monies 'nough
To clothe hands in free flask.

Gather ye your thinking cells
Reason for reason's sake be,
Treaties signed are treaties made
To curb defiled pride.

Thoughts are sure for mind,
Lend you not the ear
To every wind that bloweth by;
Tackle ye the staying work
Fore ye in chaos
Turneth defiled pride.

BITTER HERBS

I'll eat my sweets,
Drink my syrups
Come from rotted grain.
Don't care if teeth cave in;
There's burnished gold
And silvered packs
To better grind old Maude.

Nature tells when time to pull,
So I'll eat my sweets
And drink my syrups
In bare-gummed delight.

There're fakes
Like true grown enamels
Not for brushing
Each meal's end.
So let me eat my sweets
And drink my syrups
'Til sod covers me o'er.

Ate my sweets
And drank my syrups,
Golded my teeth
'Til roots died all.
Looked me better
In full plates false
But darned
Those raw, pained gums.

Changed my motto true:
Curse those sweets
And liquid sirrups;
'Tis better good will free
Than plates of false
Bickering sore-gummed me.

ALONG THE ROAD

Along the road
Children eat the sentimental touch;
When parents are olden and insecure,
The lace of sentiment
Glues a better thought
Than deeds of loving care.

Along the road
Children eat the sentimental touch
Forgotten to the year of youth again,
When pride is fierce over the fact
To bones stepping near a grave.

Along the road
Children eat the sentimental touch
As once the parent catered to its whims,
Soothing a cry settled in the sentimental touch.

When the road cease to go along
Where the children ate its touch,
None they're olden and begging the gain
Of deeds from the sentimental touch.

Children hobble and walk,
Longing the rumble of sentimental train
Since the tracks long removed
Bring not a deed to sentimental touch.

Take back the law,
        man,
Take back the law;
That's not God you saw
Out there on the unflamed haw.
Take back the law,
        man,
Take back the law.

ON REFINDING POETRY

As a thinker, I'm considered as a nut,
and as a nut, I'm thought of as a thinker—
at least that's how my clientele thinks.
I was doing fine in fiction, you know,
those novels, short stories, and such,
but when the word blew in the wind
that I wrote poetry,
that's when the thinker-nut, nut-
thinker, labeled itself on me.
I'm not hypersensitive nor am
I hyposensitive to quandary
qualitativeness. I would just
like to know what bugs the
mentality of some to label poet, or
for that matter, anyone whose words
have never been opened, much less
explored.

For those slapping on quandaries to
things not in the mind nor moment to
extricate, I would like a bit of
consideration—mind-blowing, if you
will—to make some fluctuations between
the opened and not so opened.
There is a realization, on my part,
that is, civilization stands still as
a doorknob on a knobless door until
poetry, the great fixative of
truth to fiction––fiction to truth—
is explored in all its tonal
beauty so explicatively
showing the road's begin and its
finality without end.

Surely, I remember David of his psalms.
Yes, I've read Homer, Plato, and Cicero,
even Socrates and Pliny, Seneca,
Virgil.
I loved Dante and Nibelungenlied.

Tell me if there be any who haven't read
Don Quixote or Romeo and Juliet.

Surely, there be someone who has
read Canterbury Tales.
There be some who even quote
Emerson, Hawthorne, Melville, and
yes, the Monster Conjuror, Poe.
And lest I leave out Shakespeare, I'll include him here,
though he be the any list to all feelings in a work of art,
must this litany droll on for fifty
more lines or so before the singular
message in sung in the mind?

It seems to me to be a fact;
poetry comes into its own and,
ah, yes, read and reread as
man has gone from one epoch to
another of betterment or decadence.
I cannot, not in the blossom of the
present, see whether the bud came
before or after the event of passage.
I do know, though, that poetry has always
carried that nostalgic perfume to
linger in the nostrils of each age,
to hammer and braze.

TEAR DEW ON THE ROSES

I received your roses last night
      And breathed upon them perfumed,
Though caught I was not in their delight,
      Your presence there I presumed.

If roses can love above their thorns,
      Why can breath's whisper of doom
Gore the heart with bleating horns
      To receive a measured fume?

Gone is my will. You broke my heart
      And now send roses to mend.
What be the sentence and its start
      If roses cannot defend?

Though widows sit and mourn their grief
      And smell roses day by day,
What's the mean of their sent relief
      When the heart's wasting away?

At night my dreams nightmare to you,
      And thoughts like faded roses
Do not the more perfume accrue
      As night upon day closes.

Still I hear your voice as ever
      And feign I hear you at door.
But why my love lives forever
      When you come around no more?

OUT OF THE SHADOWS

I've sat in many church pews;
While there in the quietness of my soul,
I've wondered about God's many hues
Then looked around at the very bold.

There was a people hungry for the Good News
Of a father who has a gentle scold
With a balm that ever imbues
The soul in this message ever be told.

I looked at the sons and daughters of friends,
How they romped and talked and sung;
I looked to my son, he only grins,
Many a tear from my eye he has wrung.

I tried to look to God in his heaven,
I tried to be joyful in a moment's shout;
But for me there was bread without leaven
In my heart I sprouted many a doubt.

I could not see my son's purpose in life.
I could only see what friends thought of me.
I could not see joy, but only strife
Followed me down to my raging sea.
All I heard was a drilling drum
         And a lonesome fife
Sucking the nectar of my life as a bee.
Still the hurt pains as a knife.

Along came a friend of forty-two years.
He told me things I've always known
But could not see through my tears.

He said my son, though already grown,
Was normal in his world and often hears
The voice of God and his gentle tone,
Growing my love out of its many fears.

The friend told me things already sown
In my heart burdened with many jeers.
He told me if faith could ever condone
A life without God's purpose, though in arrears,
All life would be as a sun-bleached bone
Causing death to love upon the ears.

I've prayed and searched all corners, near and far,
To come in heal my son so dear,
But all is empty as a new-washed jar
Even though heaven be so near.

My friend told me healing is soon,
But it must begin with me in heart;
For even as the sun is hot at noon,
Where does the morning and night have part?
If love should ever be wrapped in its cocoon
        And God with love knows not where to start.

When a healing comes to my son,
I'll be the most thankful by far;
But guilt shall burden me down as a gun
Since I thought God was not on par
And was only playing games with me in fun.

After my praise of God shall have run
Its course through my once raging sea,
Those drums and fife shall beat my new song
That my friend said was ever in my heart.

THE BALL I THREW IN PLAY

He threw a ball in play and said,
Oh, you great bubbling,
Swirling, spinning orb
Dancing, winding, spinning
Through heaven's sieve,
Though not in contents' bed,
Yearning not for wildness tamed,
Just some errant child
Scolding parents in discipline's stead,
Throwing fiery flaming torch
To conquered stars by discipline wed.

Ah, the joy of youthful endeavor
Bubbling mental conflagration's camera
Locked on nonpictured scene,
Swirling in bathing filmy waters
On paths of moments' nonregret.

Oh, great inertial orb,
Bubble, swirl, and spin
To gaming thrush on wing,
Flown to nonety in flight,
'Til momented resurging trail
Wears thick that once-habited veil
Broken now by energy's fail
Caught e'er within, ever wail.

Oh, good earth built in time
By playful purposeful God,
Ne'er, ne'er canst more escape
The web of steeled rod
Changing game to work.

BLUES CHASING THE WAVES

Brr-rrr-rrr-rrr, ding
Goes the alarm,
Much 'fore birds in song,
Much 'fore artist sun
Paints his cloudy masterpiece,
Much 'fore cuddling one beside
In snoozing takes his cease,
Much 'fore lovely one cried,
"Mom, just one more fleece."

First 'pon floor, toes a-freeze;
Can't find my slippers
In dark 'cause of energy squeeze.
Darn these backway zippers.
Stump my toes 'gainst doorjamb,
Cuddling one turns in bed;
Just now, couldn't give a damn,
Though he with me in wed.

Rush to room of workshop bore
There my dog in possum sleep
Done big spot, right in floor.
Unlock keep of exit peep,
Shove my dog right through door.

COME, PEACEFUL EARTH

A baby's crying wakes the star-filled morn;
No crickets on the hearth to warm the heart,
No relatives around to glow the worm
That stirs the soul to harp of spirit burn.
The straw's a cloth to whip his flesh and sear
A nerve that's close to home, but home so far
Removed, this child, mangered, from other realms,
Breaks the chord and meters David's psalms, heard,
Played, not on lute, not on lips' bland curl,
It nestles close to fires that angels stir.

He drains the lakes where springs have run and coursed.
He cleans the dew that sweats the hand with wrath.
He quiets birds that have not song to sing.
This child, this child of plead from other realms,
Quickens time and slows the dawn of will;
No warriors can win with him at helm.
This baby's cry has grown in glory now;
He's pulling stars of grass and stone to him,
They write their epitaphs in peace to him.
All world is vowed to end in peacefulness.
All earth has vowed to end in peacefulness.

SPICE FROM THE TRADE WINDS

Sing the lark beside the spring in spring
Perched aloft a budding branch,
Reigning in blossomed dress to spring's festival,
Inching its hold to life day with day—
None can fathom its trumpeted call
Gestated long before the sun comes home.

Sing, you children in the summer's summery game,
Unto that freedom nature has the dance,
Murmuring in the heart and sighing in the bones
Music like a thousand songbirds in choir,
Ending only when the magic flute of time's interval
Rumors that a time of joy ends its march.

Winging snows undulating upon frost-haired winds,
Inviting the hare and deer to tussle on flaky hills;
None but the bravery of necessity finds a call to climb,
Thankful that the snows of winter time throw their flamboyant
Envies across the throes of death-beckoning decay,
Reckoning that the song of life needs a purity thrown.

Fall time has laid summer to rest,
And winter will nip fall's quickened brush in jest,
Loathing the moment spring shall have its request.

THE GRAVES THAT WEEP
THEIR HEROES

Love is not within the world
Nor caught into the fiber of soul
When man's in constant touch with pain's churl
To make the being contrast bold.

There's love of heroes not for their deed
When death covers the deed with soil;
There's only a thought for pain's bleed
In that moment of loves despoil.

If heroes went not down to death,
There'd sooner be the villain walked
Since love denies the common breath
In this realm of love distraught.

All religions have saints all dead
Without a sing until death has come,
Then their joys are covered in pain's dread.
None their joys are sung upon the drum
Lest they be humans in joy flesh's wed.

Now come and take away that cross
Remembered not for love but for the blood,
As if joy were only the waxen floss
Whose decays were never washed by flood.

Come remember more those days before,
When heroes were our mingled ones,
Sweeping dust and smiling their sweat on floor
In this common touch of tempers and guns.

I can see my love is slain
Each time I pass those condominium tombs;
None of them beneath the soil held life in disdain,
But weary is the life within all future wombs
Until heroes can be seen before their deaths,
Then weeping shall green the grass over hero graves.

EYE VISIT

I have eyes, Lord,
The most precious gift you have given.
Didn't Adam and Eve open their eyes
          And see the destruction of their souls?
My eyes, Lord, speak the all of me,
When I talk, when I listen, when I fear,
          When I love, when I hate.
Yes, I can be the dumbest of the dumb,
          But my eyes give me away, Lord,
          And I, though the dumbest of the dumb,
Become a genius when my eyes speak me.

I must visit my eye and learn of capable me––
My tears can melt the heart of the cruelest of men;
My eyes can make saints out of sinners
          Or the reverse of heaven, Lord.
Though I be blind, my eyes still
          Cause my face to show me.
So what are my eyes, Lord,
          But the barer of my soul?
They show the height, the breadth,
          And depth of you in me.

ON WRITING FICTION OR FACT

to Isaak Roman, who taught me the basics of fiction

A subject's not a fitting, hardy choice
When words are chosen 'gainst the character
So mean, so vile, if words make him rejoice
Or change his clothes to what he never wears.
In him there must be shown some grass of earth,
Though good or bad is seen his nature drawn,
But just enough to hold his image worth
To make him what the mind has seen as brawn.
He'll taste of death or play the pardon gave
Then enter doors to solve his every whim,
Where ashes of plot has hero or knave,
Though matters not his speech, if light or grim,
      If you perceive the nature of this man,
      The story ground the nature of his sand.

JOKES

Ha, ha, ha, ha, ha-a-a-a,
Si-s-s-s-s-s-s,
Such-h-h, uh-uh-uh,
And he told her
He-ee-ee-ed-ed-ed,
Huh-h-h-h, uh-uh.

You don't
Sa-ay-ay-ay-ay.

Yeah, he told her
He'd-ed-ed-d-d,
Huh-h-h-h-uh-uh.

Is that how it
Go-o-o-o-es-es?
Ha-ha-ha-ah-ah-ah,
Si-s-s-s-s-s,
Suh-h-h-h-uh-uh,
Yea-a-a-ah-ah-ah,
And he got on the see-
Saw-aw-aw-aw-aw,
He-ee-ee-ee-e-e-e.

O-o-o-o-o-o-o-h-h-h,
I've heard that one
Befo-o-o-o-ore,
Ha-ah-ah-a-ah-ah,
Ha-a-a-ah-ah-ah.
Now let me tell you
Bout the one I heard.

And he told her
In no uncertain
Ter-er-er-er-erms,
Ha-ah-ah-ah-ah,
Uh-h-h-h-h-uh-uh,
To qui-i-i-i-it
Touc-c-c-c-ch-ching,
O-o-o-o-o-uh-uh,
Yea-a-a-ah-ah,
And you should have seen his
Fa-a-a-a-c-ce.
Suh-uh-uh-uh-uh,
H-ah-a-ha-h-aw-aw.

And he said,
I thought I would
Show you how it
Go-o-o-o-oes.
Ha-ah-ah-ah.

I've heard that one
Back when I
Wa-a-a-a-as-as,
Ha-a-a-a-ah-ah,
Ha-a-a-ah-ah-aw-aw,
A tiny boy.

GROWING PAINS

First a babe
To salve joy's wound
Fore childhood breaks the spell
Into joy again, too soon.

A babe into child,
Fretting beloved caress,
Though caress be gentle, mild,
It too, smothered 'neath a mesh,
Hid und intentions, smiled.

The child grown too soon
To paths of ladyhood,
Leaves fore'er stable dune,
Grown too small a world.

OPINION

Three tribesmen of the plains
Opened the lid of trusty trunk,
The trunk of jealousy's blains.
Tooted to soul 'til conscience drunk.
Then the action lain on hane
Sends arrow cross swift path
Towards happy hunting ground
Busy in mingled crowns of laugh
'Til Great One disembowels
Soul from sound.

SINGING THOSE
NASHVILLE SONGS

New Amsterdam, 'round yon Bedloe,
New York, 'round yon Libertine,
Castled moat proudly built
Gracing ocean harbor,
Greeted Frederic of the king,
Gifting pilgrims in strange cargo
In the year eighteen eighty four.

Couldst former foe grace this land,
This land 'round Amsterdam,
With choice huge gift, so grand,
Beaten in choicest alloy,
This lady high upon her stand.

America, America,
Built in battle scars
By red man's nonfriendly whoa,
Fearing pale ones' ewahs.

America, America,
Thought land of all arrest,
Guarded by red man's whoas,
Clouding pale ones' mental fest—
Friends to all and all a friend.

Iroquois, crushing friendship's loom
As monster of Hudson's Bedloe
Seals with powder, red balls on fire,
Chasing red man's ambush
With crashing, thundering, boom-boom.

Indian, British, French,
Test these pilgrims sore
As they in freedom's beat
Muster drafts in redress
Not wanted 'til last battle bleat.

Pilgrims born to pilgrim law,
Not escaping laws left behind,
Find friendship comes by war,
Though war felt so unkind.
Thus, duty done is duty won.

Proud this people-pilgrimed America
Dressed in loose friendship's robe,
Flowing, growing hither and yon,
Its torch so high in air
Beckons other pilgrims, fair,
In desire good-chartered law
In Declaration of Independence, love,
Though held in left wand hand.

America, America,
Great huge bejeweled crown,
Spiked oft and much,
But the sun of friendship's rays
O'ercomes the devilry of war.
United by stampeding feet
Breaking minions' hold,
No chain wrought by men
Can long this people enfold.

In this land's dark, trying times,
Frederic of the king's gift
Lights the rapidy way
With a torching light, sublime,
Bleaching darkened waves
Rippling in starry message—
We the people of the world.

Chance is as, as chance is not,
Great ships see our light.
Lowing planes right their flight.
Seeing peoples laugh at fright,
Guided by this lady of the lights.

Come, you peoples
From far worlds' realms,
To Liberty's harbor
Fathom such foundation
So boldly, solidly built.

Tread and drum to a nation,
A nation's climbing, spiraling stairs.
Glimpse this realm's freedomed shores.
Touch its feet, not wanton of tread,
'Til tread it must
The blood of friendship gone mad.
Enter its bowels of plenteous store.
Fathom its mind, ever-eyeing,
Its handheld torch
Born on friendship's freedomed anvil
Into this lady of the lights.

PLOUGH THAT DREAM

I'll pitch my tent
By Isabelle's door
And cry my tears, well spent,
For other boat of Noah.

I wake my shaking head
In dreams my day has stirred,
My purse to money fails in wed
For this beggar no ears have heard.

My dream is but a dream,
Lifting brows on shaking heads
Non-tuned to journey's gleam
To me in fool's unnerving dread.

To me, the dream is real
As lips part that blowing trill
Upwards to heaven, lying still,
In wait my weighty mail.

All dreams, all dreams flitter in air
'Til moments' unibeam
Splits the ear asunder, fair,
To opened eyes in truth, well seen.

I'm the wretched mortal
Beating drums in flurries, real,
E'en through mind's open portal
Unto wedlock's unmelded seam.

I'll catch once more that dream,
Though youth in wanton, flies
By ageing time, too soon.
I'll wake those eyes
Wrinkled by gossip's witch.
I'll still those lips, much parted,
To laughter's watch of fool.
I'll plough that dream of years
And laugh that last laugh, good.

THIS NATION

Wondrous wilderness
Of desires and thoughts
Tangled and garbled
By public sure rain,
Streaking 'cross the heavens
Enlightening the flames.

As the cannons in cloudy-land
Burst the thoughtful duress
And test that sword of light
With scaring boomerang,
The heavens in sunlit fest
Brings this nation's scabbard
In friendship's smiling rest.

Oh, wondrous wilderness
Of desires and thoughts,
Dress now those wounds
Of nations in torn boughs.
Sing now those songs of freedom
Long in hide this peopled world.

Oh, wondrous wilderness
Of desires and thoughts,
Cease now thy symphony
And drum thy unison call
To children of nationed world
Not of this nation's freedom ball.

Come now, oh nationed America,
Ride this wondrous wilderness,
Bridge future friendship pool,
Trumpet out this world of fear,
Drum into the half-shapened mold,
Freedom's wind of desires and thoughts,
March on, conquer the warring sword
Tilted not to freedom's light.

'Tis then, 'tis then, oh nationed America,
'Twill not be thy song
From mountains to sea
Nor from sea to shining sea,
But 'twill be the rhythm of song
Poured out by all colors of skin
And sung within all hearts of men.

CASTLED BANKS

I come to my pleasure's end,
My trail's beaten path,
To pond lying downwind.
Came I not for a bath,
Just a want to bend,
Me with my rod,
Hook, and sinker.

Came I to King Pike's home,
Who welcomed me not within.
I quaked his roofing shingles.
He shouted,
"Oh, what a sin."
I for a moment doubted,
Me with my rod,
Hook, and sinker.

No talk was heard
In King Pike's kingdom,
Only faking blows to hook,
Making my nerves hum
Some reciped cook,
Me with my rod,
Hook, and sinker.

Waited and waited
Long minutes, long;
Though my hook's baited,
King Pike knew something wrong,
Seeing my rod,
Hook, and sinker.

I in hypnotic trance,
As mind laid eyes to rest,
I popped up as wand began to dance.
Has King Pike my hook caressed
As I held my pants?
I pulled hard,
Hard against nature's winker,
Me with my rod,
Hook, and sinker.

Smelly curds hung in air,
My hand danced,
Danced with angle's flair.
My tongue, pouch, and eyes entranced
As suddenly, much too suddenly,
My wand stopped in dance, bare.
I cried, cried in cursing, fair,
"Fool, fool, fool.
Why me with rod,
Hook, and sinker?"

TIME IN EVERBIDE

What's my worth?
Loving hands ask,
Fondling me at birth.
What's his till in flask?

Strangers soothe my fitful cry
And walk the ground I'm to tread.
They're on that ever-rocking train,
Rocked ever in the bye,
Plied by dreams others said
Love plays e'er to sigh
In watch a cribbing bed.

What's my worth?
Others ask as I in play
Shoot my marbles forth in mirth
And command not obey
Nor measure time in girth
That tendered loving way.

What's my worth?
This mind asks me oft
In sing my place in berth
As plush feathers drown my loft
And opinion works my surf
Till days and twilight's bucking craft
Stirs this mind in awe.

I, in wait, natured happy song
Blown in winds gusting youth,
Others say much too long.
'Tis but I in search of truth
Held in lessoned tuning tong,
Till life doth say with searching sooth.
I've found my worth
O'er the coverlets of wrong.

LIFT THE SILT FROM STREAM

I look o'er my years of dream
Thrown to yen's trusting mare,
Stampeding bounteous stream
To oceans, calm and wide,
Made by my too-trusting will.

This mind looking, still,
Through that windowed pane,
Calms my fretting feet
Standing angry open door
As my hands
Lift the silt from stream,
Paining eyes weeping tears
In ask,
Why the teaching bird
Flies thy home no more.

Come drink my gall
Sopped with pity's bread
Whilst demon of self-reliance
Rapes this feinting bed
Bought from apathy's store.

From my windowed pain
I look that stream
Began in ester's labor
Wed to promised dream,
Slowly silting road of life.

That cup of youth,
Filling e'er to mellowed years,
Teases pride running fast
O'er fair reason's meres
Down ester's growing stream.

From ester's foundation built,
Through present dooming stoop
The windows of labor's house
Look the wonder's view
O'er the staling table spread
To dream of lifting silt from stream.

The ester's leaf looks
The present's wonder
Whilst that future dream
Unfolds its tale too soon,
Yet my chair sits in place.

My chair in place does sit
As the mind in wondering goes,
Where's the frosting, piled heap,
O'er the pall of labor's cake?
Where's the feasting table spread?
Where's that purse on labored hip
In purchase necessity store?

All, all wondered pain
Strikes the eyes in tearing bath,
Shying flint's all sparkled path,
In wait not the stream's high tide,
Higher by silt's resting bed
Lifted not by labor's resting chair,
Wondering e'er in wondered pain.

A QUAINTLY CACKLE

Quaint old towns
Reflect our turbulent woes
Gone down, gone down,
To mirroring pool.

Sugarcanes and licorice
Haunt our nostril-led air,
Paining nerves in air, delish,
Beckoning soul to unkind snare
As pavement glues feet in desire.

Musty smells and acrid smoke
Pull hard 'gainst elements up there,
Cringing bowels in want of soak,
Tearing mouth with gurgling flair.

NEW BREED BEGETS NO BREED

I don't have time
To get my man,
So my man gets me.

I don't have time
To sign forever papers,
So me and my man
Live on in sweet harmony.

I don't have time
To share my love,
So I call Mr. Abortion.

I don't have time
To light the oven,
So I'm bound for quick-food out.

I don't have time
To pretty my looks,
Just don a wig
And damn the looks.

I've got time
To sex my man,
To live in house with him,
To swell my womb,
To fix favorite dish,
To set frizzy wig,
But darned
If I'll waste my time
In obligations expected of me.

So sob, sob, sob,
Goes God's religion.
Bang, bang, bang,
Shouts the civil gun.
Gulp, gulp, gulp,
Goes down my pills.
Ha, ha, ha,
Death laughs at me.

Oh, fleeing moment
Of hanging life,
I believe.
I'll do the law.
Break my habit
If death lets go of me.

FALLEN BY THE LICKS

Chain this garland 'round my head
Won in bribes and peasant smiles.
All is well on fronts, met.
Shake not boughs laden down
'Fore this ruler bides his time.

My garland, to me, so very proud,
Won in bribes and peasant smiles,
Lay on my head very well
'Til peasant friends in ask of me,
Is my chain on ankles sore
To fret my soul in every time
On my fair harp of golden bribes?

My fair garland in lay of head
Wilts one flower won
By riches bribes and peasant smiles,
Drops all petals 'round my feet
'Cause one in friendship's swing
Shook the boughs laden down,
Plunging me down, down, down,
Crushed, fallen by the locks.

This my place in history be,
Swallowed by riches' bribes,
Frowned down in peasant smiles,
As I onwards walk nevermore
Through the open water gates
Unto consciented nation's home.

OH, LONELY SIGHT

My tide came in,
Bringing its load to me,
Pounding its drooling words
O'er the whited olden sands
Washed each day in each day's wash
In the creel of nature ship.

I wondered among
The gathered treasures, all,
In awestruck thought
Mementos drew me down,
Down to play in the sea.

My hand reached out
And held the past
Of battered, once-trusty craft.
My tide in whisper
Told my anxious, listening ear
A board makes not
The path of a soul, as free.

Oh, lonely sight,
This dead green grass
Hugging one board, last,
Lost on the deep of the sea,
That buoyant, salty, briny sea
Gathering all worshippers, lost,
To one, oh, lonely sight.

RESOUND THE ECHO

The Bible resounds with an echoing command,
"By the sweat of thy brow shall you gather by hand."
Along came lords and took over the land
Of the highest esteem they were thought as grand
While the tillers of the soil honored the sand,
Making it rich with the manure they panned.

Resound the echo and vibrate labor's good hoe;
There are still new fields and lawns to mow.

Always afield from morning 'til evening dusted;
Something had to be done with their money all rusted.
The traders and merchants couldn't be trusted.
There came guilds of craftsmen all encrusted
With hopes that the soils-man would spend until busted.
Nay! Nay! The soils-man became all disgusted
When Columbus and explorers brought
back a gold they lusted.
This the beginning of labor's tears a-cussed;
Machines became dearer than sweat all dusty.

Resound the echo (etc.).

Labor cried in the pan once loaded with gold,
"Nay!" they said, "Machines will not our slavery hold."
Boss man said, "You work until you fold,
My competitors have ten-timed my goal.
You're fired! A woman shall take your droll."
The slave looked back and spit the boss in the eye.
"Egypt! Egypt! Made a people cry and so am I,
But you'll learn an employee is worth his rye
Or the purse of product will drain you dry."

Resound the echo (etc.)

Many had theories about labor's great pun
When came Aquinas (1200), Calvin (1500), Smith (1700),
Recardo (1700), and Karl Marx (1800) had fun;
They said, "Labor is the source of all values—in the run."
Management said, "Ha! We still buy your bun!"

Resound the echo and vibrate labor's good hoe;
There are still new fields and lawns to mow.

There were hoe cakes still in the fire
When Samuel, the Gompers (1850–1924), stepped from the mire.
He said, "There must be a better cause for hire
Other than whips and stripes and muscles of wire!"

Resound the echo and vibrate labor's good hoe;
There are still new fields and lawns to mow!

He, the Gompers, chose a few with lips of dew
To speak in Washington's graveside mew.
Management said, "We must go there too,
Gompers brews too tasty a stew!"
Many followed this lad from the mire, as savior new,
Labor formed in unions as equals too.

Resound the echo (etc.)

Laws were made less bitter, few by few,
When government saw the rose budding as reason true.
The railroads men (1926) kicked all things askew;
They bargained at a collective table gathering up the dew.
Uncle Sam in '35 extended the call to all.
He said in '38, no worker must go to bed late

Unless time and a half be after the bell's call.
In the mines of '46, health and welfare was rebate,
While at steel in '49, a pension wrapped the shawl.
The next year, workers on those cars drank to COLA's ball.
'55 was a good year to guarantee wages as update,
But management called it SUB since labor torpedoed the wall.

Resound the echo and vibrate labor's good hoe;
There are still new fields and lawns to mow!

O glorious history so laboriously won,
When will we honor these saints as over their graves we run?
Union meetings are attended as one scared of a gun,
Apathy and disregard labor used to shun
Now in the local it is as a lighthearted ton
With union leaders getting thanks in the form of a dun.
In this day when money and credit is tight,
Oh! Will mercy rise up in the night
After management has stolen our good fight!

Resound the echo and vibrate labor's good hoe;
There are still new fields and lawns to mow!

On into the future, our light must burn bright,
Yesterday's squalls were nothing
compared to the oncoming fight.
The stars shall fall, the sun and moon shall
cease their light;
This is when labor shall have won its right—
It's right to be the new stars, the new sun, and moon.
Labor will create its own buffoons
In robots, automation, and space travel to galaxies soon,
Spurring civilization away from earth's sand dune
In this treaty of space labor has hewn.

Resound the echo and vibrate labor's good hoe;
There are still new fields and lawns to mow.

Let the earthquakes shake the enemy's domain,
Labor! Labor shall regally reign!
Labor shall music the realms in a joyous refrain!
Labor! Labor! Labor shall feel no pain!
It is labor making its own sunshine and rain!
By the sweat of brow and gather of hand,
      LOOK!
WATCH!   and   KNOW!
Labor has made a man!
Labor has its woman in the same good pan!

THE RACE DAY'S END

Mr. Dalton rode his horse
Out of pasture at a trot;
The trail was muddy,
But horse failed not the trot.

Howling Howell
Picked the prettiest steed
Out of pasture he galloped by
The horse with a trot.

The galloping horse
Huffed and puffed and huffed
Three quarters through
From feeding on locoweed.

Howling Howell dug the spurs
Into flesh, blood, and bone,
But the horse only ate the burrs
And listened to the riders' moans.

The horse with trot
Went galloping through the gate
Past the pretty broken steed;
Howling Henry soon found a fate
'Twas but the civil conscience
Putting a horse to shed.

Now the Dalton shakes the Howling hand
And thanks the Henry
For beating too loud, the band;
He chides the tearful Henry
From the mansion, so grand,
"Next time you mount the chimney, Henry,
Plug the hole with sensible sand."

PROUD HUMILITY

Oh, quake my eyes in wonder
To life's times in oft,
Like billowed waves,
Frightfully tossing and churning
The mind in full-blown wind.

Oh, quake my eyes in wonder
To life's times in seldom beat
As flesh in storm tossed craft
Forgets the humble tune
Of the mind in full-blown wind.

Oh, quake my eyes in wonder
To life's times in always,
Flirting in that love of spirit
Though compassed not by needle, strong.

My ship need not the straightway course
Of the mind in full-blown wind
'Til mine eyes once quaked in wonder
Sees life's time in always,
Just mine billowed waves
Crashing on my storm-tossed mind.

THE YEARLING STAR

An unknown brother
  Came forth in peace,
His honor for country
  Gave his soul its need.
His desires of country,
Well thought and forged,
Lent new and brighter flame
To the ruled thought unruled.
  The name of prophet
   He would not,
Only called as servant
  To servant the servient.
He the great tiller
Of his home state's soil,
  The blossom of the South,
The South's aromatic bergamot.

Oh, did he chase
  That fear from soul
With peaceful, engendered smile
  In beg a nation's trust,
Spit at,
  Spurned,
   And cajoled
For words from truth's mini jar?
He won not by millions,
  Though those millions
He trustingly understood,
  Whose fear was change.
Now this farmer,
  Yesterday's unknown,
Treads a nationed stair
Remodeled, refurbished
  By love's humble tone.

All nations gained
       By America's star.
His enlightened light
          shining
From the greatest light
          Known.
His first reign saw peace,
Though not cold
         Nor hot,
Only glowing embers
          Trampled
By two centuries
Of gain and rulers' begot.

His second reign
Brought prophecy true,
The lamb with lion
Plowed all fields, anew.

He,
       The yearling star.
He,
The Jim of a nation's ring.
He,
      The Carter,
          The cotter pin.

PAINT FROM A POEM

The poet   poetess,
        not only feels life;
He,   she,
Sees life poured from a cup
Not as poisoned dregs of strife,
Though strife oft the topic be.

The poet,   poetess
Paints with etch upon the mind,
Change,   she
Changes the wall's wallpaper
        each time
The poem is read beside another
        moment flowered in time.

When there be not
        poets   and   poetesses,
There be life remaining stale
        to dregs in cup
With poisoned dregs of strife
Await the lift of another cup
        that
He   she,
        poet   poetess,
Splashed and messed life all up.

WHY POETRY SHOULD BE READ

Old taboos are hard to die,
At least in the city of male
Regarding poetry, as they lie,
But of that gender, grossly male,
More the poets did classic-fy
Their shortened verse of tale.

In those days of farmer in the dale
And chivalry was spirited with rye
Or sea captains busied their ships of sail,
'Twas not time for book to eye
Lest education caught one frail
And strength of male would sooner die.

Though where a woman of gentileness
Blessed her scent-o-spice in cooking,
She learned the art of love and kiss
From the poems in her booking,
And she lured the male with her twist
Taught by Chaucer, all a-looking.

Thus a poem has its art,
Leaving a reader to give it life;
There is strength of mind from the start
To shorten details of strife.

GANTRY PLANK

Christen me lovely names
Spoke not oft by tongue
In each days wag
For I'm the ploughman
Of the mighty deep

'Spensive though I come
'Spensive though I go,
'Spensive not I believe
Than mile-high pillars
Spanning chasm's breach,
For I'm the ploughman
Of the mighty deep.

Great, high, mighty named
Great, high, mighty blamed
Though sciented alloy,
Screaming in better dress,
Grows me old
Yet not christened be.
I'm the ploughman
Of the mighty deep.

My captain scolds me oft
Though I not cause be.
My rudders go in path
Helmsman lays for me.
Antibodies salve my wounds
And sew my searing faults.
I'm the ploughman
Of the mighty deep.

Built for pleasure,
Built for war,
Built for stardom,
Built for whale's jaw,
Built of list,
Built for lean,
Built for beggar,
And built for queen.
I'm the ploughman
Of the mighty deep.

See my wake,
See my steam,
See the waves
Claw me clean.
See me proud
In nations' 'steem.
I'm the ploughman
Of the mighty deep.

ODE TO A MIDGET

Tiny little mite
Gladdening every heart
Though thy little heart
Piteously broke
By giant's scathing dart.

Tiny little feet
Braving giant's land
For giant's laugh
Though not in askance,
Lacking giant's gene.

Tiny little hands
Making tiny little waves
Etched in giant's glance,
'Tis you 'pon life's stance
Riding horse of smiles.

THIS HABIT OF MINE

Hold my hands, my love,
That keeps them in place.

Hold my hands, my love,
I've no will but thine.

Hold my hands, my love,
Keep mind's camera clear.

Hold my hands, my love,
Fly the dove out of hat.

Hold my hands, my love,
'Til vows said in church.

Hold my hands, my love,
'Tis but habit of mine.

PRIDE

Rank grow the violets
In some memoried paths:
  Swamp violets,
  Meadow violets,
  Alpine violets
Share same-natured blood
Though kindred, like class,
Class, the enviable vial,
Better the mounds of violets
Than putrid worms.

SATISFIED

My love's in the kitchen,
Making a tasty treat.
My son's in the bathtub,
Washing warts off his feet.
My daughter's at the glass,
Making mud pies on her face.
My pet's in the brake grass,
Smelling the lowly mace.
I'm in the heavenward way,
Pondering such family grace.
The Trinity's in obey;
This family has good taste.
The world's at a mob gay,
Making things well graced.

THERE'S AN UNITAS DEUS

This is God's world:
The world is made for people,
People are made for God,
God is made for marriage,
Marriage is made
For woman and man.

Woman and man
Are made for babies,
Babies are made
Into boys and girls.

Boys are made for frogs,
Girls are made for cats,
Frogs are made for warts,
Cats are made for birds.

Birds are made for butterflies,
Butterflies are made for blossoms,
Blossoms are made for fruit,
Fruit is made for insects,
Insects are made for nothing,
Just to make the cycle
Begin its cycled rebirth.

Worry not, my child of the world,
This eating, drinking, and playing
Killing, encroaching, and times
The Creator takes his leave.

Parents protect not the child
When home is left far behind.
Grow up, my child of the world,
Brains are made for thinking,
Loving, soothing, and laughing
To the things God
Wants each child
To return opened to him.

There's an Unitas Deus
With a father for just.
There's an Unitas Deus
With a son in loving must.
There's an Unitas Deus
With a spirit
To tickle our minds with mirth.

THIS PROBLEM OF MINE

I placed my hand
In the hand of him
Who loved my mother.
I placed my hand
In the hand of him
Too blind to see me.

He just talked to the doctor
As mother shed her tears.
He told of the world's
Problems too big for him.

So I placed my hand
In the hand of him
Who loved my mother.
I placed my hand
In the hand of him
Too blind to see me.

The doctor said,
"This gonna be
A healthy baby,
Someday he'll make
The world a fine place, maybe."

So I placed my hand
In the hand of him
Who loved my mother.
I placed my hand
In the hand of him
Too blind to see me.

Two lovers in hand, a kiss:
A house too big for luck,
A car each year
To sell the product.

So I placed my hand
In the hand of him
Who loved my mother.
I placed my hand
In the hand of him
Too blind to see me.

The gas, the food, the wavy wires.
The dues, the tax, and hated liars.
Too much, too much
For support of baby criers.

A NATION BUILDS

Those names penned beside
        crushing forces,
        wars,
        petitions,
        civil-religious strife
may be hard and long on decipher
to the eye,
        screening,
        screaming,
"Whose hand in life is this,
creating me and a nation born—
yes, born—into a newer day,
into this constitutional
        freedom,
This Adamic day, reborn?
        All hail,
        The constitution!

ROCKING AND EYEING

There's polo and golf,
Base and basketballs,
Soccer and footballs;
Oh my, where will it end?
I only named a few.

There's hockey and skeets,
Skiing and skating too,
There's boxing and wrestling
Fishing with many tools,
There's track and vaulting,
And weightlifting fools.

There're spectators in millions
With seems nothing to do,
There's books to be read
And minds taught anew.
There're friends to be said,
They like pool too.

There're taverns with beer heads
As monkey shine accrues;
There're plays and shows fed
With wordy giggling due.

There're maids in waiting for wed
As grooms sip another dew,
While friendly slaps
Fall on Mother and Dad.
My world's quite busy;
Hope yours is too.

I'm paged to rocking chair,
Just rocking and eyeing,
Laughing and crying
To the things people do.

I'm mostly seventy-eight,
Can't wait for seventy-nine
Years to satiate,
Doing things people do.

TALE E'ER SO TRUE

Oh, prophetic vision
Lain in brambles long
'Ere timely time's derision
Sings its tale in truthful song
In metered-verse decision,
Though partial yet not wrong.

In visionary's dream, groped,
Strife the first in tale
Long in wait for sober day
As legions of diversity's throne
Begin the way of nonworship wail
Plied to cries of hushed unborn,
Dried e'er fore the pruner's hook,
Saves tree of deadly wound.

In wake aft dreamland glide,
My visionary saw old senile men
Rather maimed in death's valley of pride
Wage their wars and die with grin
Through crusted tears long since dried.

Nonshaken by thrust of head,
This beast-ghosting dreamland's vision
Reaps harvest none for future's shed,
Leaning to elements mostly won,
Though leathery bats increase their bed
As pestilence cries mostly done.

Come you now all creeds of men,
All racing bloods and origins all,
Pick you worms from centuries' grave
That grave nontriumphant at his call,
Whose bugle's only heard by his friends
Playing tune of tapping call to roll
As mind no longer tends the flesh
In bathwaters ne'er so clear.

Hush! Hush, my beloved ones,
Hear my vision's ringing bell
Tolling in the holy branch
For cedar's oil forevermore.

BORN TO GRIEVE THE CAISSON'S RUT

Born to elements in changing structure,
Fighting blood's alchemetic vial
Wed to cells' quick-changing fashion
This body lives awhile
In death's cresting deltoid tide.

Infancy's wisdom sitting in rocking chair,
Quietly, nimbly hides the crush of time
'Til chains a crocheted quilt
Sadistically smothers last loop in hand.

Once this mantle lovingly laid
O'er placid soul, living, dying und'neath,
All tells well to mental crop
'Til pulling energy on high
Beckons vial unload itself
In ne'er-filling spirit pool.

Great and small living cells left behind
Ponders knell of once-beautied bell
And finger eye for one last tear
As wind of conscience deftly bends
Tale of tear sadly making last amends.

Body born to forgetting mound
In caisson's empty yet filling rut
Wetted indeed by short-lived tear
Dried to the morrow's fresh-washed cloth,
Beginning life's cycle o'er once again
'Til spirit one more soul does call,
Called indeed to grieve the caisson's rut.

Until the morrow brings a fresh-poured rain,
There is grief for all but the one who's lain
As the corporal beneath the caisson's pall
Birthed indeed to that heavenly call,
But lonely in the forgetting mound
As nerves dull that time of sound
When grief had its gall to stall
The flight of a soul to help one and all
Away from the pounding caisson's rut.

Good day! Hope you enjoy the day's blessing.

I herewith give you an insight into me as an author.

I was born in North Carolina. I moved with my parents when two years old to a farm in Virginia and graduated from Kenbridge High School.

My work history is quite varied. My work history includes: Dupont, Army, grocery clerk, greenhouse, Reynolds Metals Company and with an electrical contractor.

I became interested in literature in the eighth grade. Since then I've been writing poetry, short stories, plays aqnd essays. If it had not been for Xlibris publishing company urging me to publish my works, they would still be in storage boxes until today.

Edwards Brothers Malloy
Thorofare, NJ USA
October 31, 2014